THE
SPY
IN
THE
RUSSIAN
CLUB

THE
SPY
IN
THE
RUSSIAN
CLUB

Ronald Kessler

How Glenn Souther Stole
America's Nuclear War Plans
and Escaped to Moscow

Charles Scribner's Sons
New York

Charles Scribner's Sons
Macmillan Publishing Company
866 Third Avenue, New York, NY 10022
Collier Macmillan Canada, Inc.

Library of Congress Cataloging-in-Publication Data
Kessler, Ronald.
    The spy in the Russian club : how Glenn Souther stole America's
nuclear war plans and escaped to Moscow/Ronald Kessler.
        p. cm.
    Includes bibliographical references.
    ISBN 0-684-19116-4
    1. Souther, Glenn Michael, 1957?–1989. 2. Espionage, Soviet—
United States. 3. Spies—Soviet Union—Biography. 4. Spies—
United States—Biography. 5. Soviet Union. Komitet
gosudarstvennoĭ bezopasnosti—Biography. 6. United States—
History—1969–   7. Nuclear weapons—United States—History.
I. Title.
E839.8.K47   1990
327.12′092—dc20   89-29778
                                                             CIP

Macmillan books are available at special discounts for bulk purchases
for sales promotions, premiums, fund-raising, or educational use.
For details, contact:

Special Sales Director
Macmillan Publishing Company
866 Third Avenue
New York, NY 10022

10 9 8 7 6 5 4 3 2 1

Designed by Jack Meserole

PRINTED IN THE UNITED STATES OF AMERICA

For Dr. Myer M. Kessler, my stepfather,
and in memory of
Dr. Ernest Borek, my father

Acknowledgments

I N M Y twenty-five years as a journalist, this was one of the most difficult projects I have ever undertaken. The subject was espionage, always fraught with secrecy. But what made this investigation particularly difficult was the fact that the case in question was still open and had not been prosecuted. In addition, the investigative agencies had bungled, giving them no incentive to talk. Indeed, given the magnitude of the damage to national security and the paucity of publicity, it is clear the government covered up the case to hide embarrassment.

The cover-up extended beyond the government. Some of those who knew of Glenn Souther's spy activities before he defected wanted to hide their knowledge. Others were embarrassed that they had known him at all. They not only would not cooperate but wanted their names kept out of the book.

Then there was the surprise ending, one that made headlines around the world but would make it even more difficult to obtain answers to some questions.

I am therefore particularly grateful to those who made the book possible. First, as always, was my family. My wife, Pamela W. Kessler, not only gave me the emotional support that is critical to writing a book but also served as a wise colleague, discussing each turn of events and reading and editing the manuscript. Through their love and understanding, my children, Greg V. Kessler and Rachel Kessler, were pillars of support. Because of her writing ability, Rachel was able to contribute colorful descriptions of key characters from photographs.

My agent, Julian Bach, gave his usual strong support and wise counsel. My editor, Edward T. Chase, provided encouragement and enthusiasm at critical junctures.

Several friends in the intelligence community and my friend Daniel M. Clements read the manuscript and pointed out areas that could be improved. Each made extremely helpful suggestions that were incorporated in the book.

Those who consented to be interviewed have my thanks. Because Americans have so little knowledge of how espionage really works, they often miss the telltale signs that would tip them to spy operations. By letting people know the kinds of activity Souther engaged in, those who were interviewed performed a public service.

While some cannot be named, those who were interviewed or otherwise helped out include:

Jon Berryman, Timothy L. Biter, Nancy Brock, William E. Burrows, Donald F. Burton, E. King Butterworth, Katherine Byrd, Kimerly J. Cain, Lieutenant Bruce A. Cole, Cindy (described in a footnote to Chapter 8), Joyce Cleveland, William Cline, Sheila Coffin, and Captain William H. Cracknell.

Also Roger L. Depue, Mark J. Dickinson, Patrizia Di Palma,

Rebecca Bendixon, Dorianna Dobbins, Clifford E. Duggan, Jr., David A. Eastwood, Commander John A. Fahey, Lieutenant General Lincoln D. Faurer, Seymour Feshbach, Theresa Fisher, and Robert A. Fitch.

Also Deborah Fisher, William N. Goodbar, Robert J. Graham, Jr., Frances J. Hassencahl, David Hauser, Mike Hentzel, Ebba R. Hierta, Frances Higger, Sharon K. Hodge, Lina Holzer, and Raymond Humphries.

Also Jeffrey W. Junkens, Karen A. Kinne, Robin Kinstler, Danine D. Klein, Boris Konny, Cynthia Kotulak, Dennis Leighton, Darcie A. Long, Andrea L. Looke, Lieutenant Ellen M. Lucas, and Mark F. Lynch.

Also Lori Manik, Philip R. Melangton, Jr., Dr. Leonid I. Mihalap, Dr. Murray S. Miron, Dr. Giuseppe Motti, Carol Norton, Cheryl D. Oberg, Phillip A. Parker, William Petsas, Christopher L. Philips, and Amy S. Rodenburg.

Also Svetlana (Lana) Sapozhnikov, Betty Seagraves, Shelley Seagraves, Rear Admiral Donald M. "Mac" Showers, Jon S. Smith, Angelo Souther, Timothy Souther, Judge Robert W. Stewart, and Mitchell J. Stout.

Also Scott O. W. Sublett, Brenda Sweeney, John J. Sweeney, Frederick E. Talbott, Major General Edmund R. Thompson, Ann Urband, Edna Vance, the Rev. Mary C. (Missy) Vance, James Vitkus, James Vitkus, Jr., John C. Wagner, Carolyn Weiser, and Dr. Issa R. Zauber.

THE SPY IN THE RUSSIAN CLUB

1

If you wish,
I shall rage on raw meat;
or, as the sky changes its hue,
I shall grow irreproachably tender:
not a man, but a cloud in trousers!

—VLADIMIR MAYAKOVSKY, "A Cloud
in Trousers"

ON JUNE 27, 1989, the Soviet army newspaper *Red Star* reported some bizarre news. An obituary, signed by the ruling committee of the KGB, noted that Soviet intelligence officer Mikhail Yevgenyevich Orlov had died suddenly at the age of thirty-two.

Identifying him as a "staff member of the KGB," the obituary said Orlov had lived a "short but brilliant and interesting life which was totally devoted to the struggle for removing the threat of nuclear catastrophe hanging over humanity and working for a better future for mankind.[1]

"Over a long period of time, he carried out responsible special assignments and made a major contribution to ensuring the state security of the Soviet Union. This struggle demanded enormous personal courage and expenditure of all his physical and spiritual strength," the obituary said.

Calling his death "an enormous loss for all of us," the obit-

3

uary concluded, "The bright memory of the courageous intelligence officer, a convinced internationalist, a gifted, sympathetic, and a kind person, will remain forever in the grateful hearts of the Soviet people."

In parentheses, the obituary identified Orlov as Glenn Michael Souther, an American.

Just two years earlier, Souther, a U.S. Navy photographer with a top-secret clearance, had defected from the United States and sought asylum in the Soviet Union. The wording of his obituary suggested that Souther had been a mole—introduced into the United States as a teenager under deep cover. News organizations assumed from the obituary that he had been a KGB plant.

"If he in fact was an illegal or deep-cover agent infiltrated into the U.S., a technique which Moscow has been highly successful at using since World War II, he could not have been older than eighteen when sent in," a Reuters story said. "It was at that age that he enlisted in the U.S. Navy. Although it was possible that he had been given the name Orlov after coming to the Soviet Union, it would have been against past Soviet practice to record his death under an assumed name and not his real one."

There was pandemonium in the U.S. intelligence community as everyone with knowledge of the case scrambled to find out what this could mean. Ever since Souther disappeared in 1986, both the Federal Bureau of Investigation and the Naval Investigative Service (NIS) had been conducting an intensive, secret investigation of his activities and background. He had been assigned to one of the most sensitive posts in the Pentagon, a naval intelligence center in Norfolk, Virginia, known as FICEURLANT (pronounced "fickerlant"). If in fact he had removed material from the facility and given it to the Soviets, he would have been one of the most important spies in U.S. history.

4

In light of that, the Soviet article raised troubling questions: Who were Souther's real mother and father? Were the people who claimed to be his parents Americans or people posing as Americans? Where was he in fact born? Did anyone know him as a child? If so, was it really he or another boy? And if he had been an American, why were the Russians seeking to portray him as a Soviet?

Consternation turned to panic as investigators realized that the Defense Investigative Service, in investigating Souther before he received a top-secret clearance, had failed to check with the town clerk in Hammond, Indiana, to see if he had a birth certificate on file—a basic requirement in such checks. As it turned out, the FBI had subsequently verified his birth, but the filing could easily have been a ruse. In infiltrating illegals or moles into the United States, the Soviets commonly use the name of a person who has died. In that case, the only way to verify through records that a person is the same as the one listed on a birth certificate is to compare his footprint with the footprint on file with the hospital where he was born.

Meanwhile, the confusion created endless stories about Souther and his background.

"Our records show he was born in Hammond, and that he went to school in Munster from kindergarten through most of high school," James Bawden, the assistant principal of Munster High School, told Reuters.

When asked about the possibility that Souther might have been planted by the Soviets as a mole at an early age, Bawden replied, "No, no, I wouldn't think so."[2]

A mini-feud broke out between Souther's two Russian professors at Old Dominion University in Norfolk, Virginia, where Souther had learned Russian before his defection. Speculating that Souther was a mole, Leonid I. Mihalap told Reuters that he was an average Russian student—except for one final, stunning thirty-page handwritten paper, in virtually flawless Russian.

"I'm very seriously inclined to think that he could have been a native speaker," the Soviet-born professor said.

But John A. Fahey said he was not a mole. The wire services quoted him as saying he had helped Souther to polish the paper, which was submitted for a statewide Russian essay contest and was not supposed to be submitted for college credit.

"The paper was very weak," Fahey said. "We corrected just about all the glaring errors."[3]

"He struggled, particularly in the beginning," Fahey said. "In the end he had a reasonable proficiency but his grammar still wasn't that good."

The following day, no less a figure than Vladimir A. Kryuchkov, the chief of the KGB, told reporters in Moscow that Souther had been recruited early in his naval career but that he was an American. He said Souther had committed suicide on June 22, 1989, and had been buried in Moscow June 26 with full military honors as a KGB major. Souther's mother and brother went to Moscow for the funeral and saw Souther buried near the legendary Kim Philby, who spied for the KGB from within MI6, Britain's secret intelligence service.

"His nervous system could not stand the pressure," Kryuchkov said. "This was a tragic thing. . . . He had long displayed a nervous state of mind. He was a very gifted, emotional, caring, sensitive person, and he could be easily hurt. We cannot blame anyone for his death."[4]

Addressing the question of whether he was a Soviet mole infiltrated into the West, the KGB chief said, "He was an American, born in Indiana. Don't give us too much credit."

Kryuchkov also revealed that Souther had a Soviet wife and an eighteen-month-old daughter.

"We can be quite open about this," he said. "We have our spies, and you have yours."

Kryuchkov said Souther had left behind a suicide note thanking the KGB and the Soviet government for what they had done for him. He said Souther had come to the KGB as a result of his political convictions.

"I must also say that it was a great personal loss," he said. "I had met him several times."

Because of the "massive interest" of Soviet citizens, he said, more details would be reported in the near future.

Shortly thereafter, on July 1, 1989, *Pravda* praised Souther as a spy who had access to "the most secure and valuable documents disclosing plans of the U.S. Navy's operations in a nuclear war against the Soviet Union and other socialist countries."[5]

In addition, the newspaper article said, he had access to U.S. space intelligence.

"Glenn many times was present at operational meetings where officers with tranquil composure discussed plans for the use of two to three nuclear bombs in order to terrorize the enemy," the Soviet newspaper said. "They pointed out on the map plans as if using a soup ladle on one's dinner tablecloth. No one has the nerves to stand this. He clenched his fists and his brain fixed attentively as he compared details and selected the most important.

"Souther did everything to help the forces of peace," *Pravda* concluded. "He occupies a place in the line of KGB intelligence agents to which such outstanding soldiers of 'the invisible front' as Kim Philby and George Blake belonged." These men created conditions so that "atom bombs do not fall on Soviet cities," the newspaper said.

Philby had supplied the Soviets with information for nearly

thirty years and was responsible for the deaths of a number of agents working for the British. Like Philby, Blake spied for the KGB from within the British secret intelligence service and betrayed a number of Western agents to the Soviets. Both defected to the Soviet Union, and Philby was made a KGB general before he died in 1988. Blake attended Philby's funeral.[6]

Pravda quoted from Souther's suicide note: "Justice demands that you hear my last words. I do not regret our relationship. It was a long-standing one, and it helped me grow as a person. I wish to be buried in the uniform of an officer of the KGB."

In an unusually candid statement, *Pravda* attributed Souther's suicide to the hardships of Soviet life and the pressures of his years under cover.

"Of course, when he arrived on Soviet soil, he did not find all the things that he had dreamed of," the Communist Party newspaper said. "He failed to understand, for example, how it is possible to go shopping and not find what you are looking for."

Reading over the original obituary, it was easy to see how the Soviets, in their eagerness to lionize Souther, would inadvertently portray him as one of their own. The obituary was written more as a eulogy than as a newspaper story. Yet one could not help but marvel at its effect. Because of its whiff of mystery, the story had taken on a life of its own. Almost as if a brilliant New York publicist were orchestrating it, the articles about Souther continued for the next week.

If the cause of death had appeared in the obituary in the first place, there would have been no follow-up stories reporting how he died. But because the obituary said he had died "suddenly," reporters pursued the story even more aggressively in an effort to piece together the puzzle.

In Washington, meanwhile, the U.S. government covered up what had happened. This is standard operating procedure in espionage cases, and the blanket of silence falls not only on the press but the courts as well. Over the years, the Justice Department has had to fight repeatedly to prosecute American spies because the intelligence agencies have insisted that doing so would give away too many secrets. Yet the very reason for the prosecutions is that the Soviets already have found out the secrets in question.

At the time, there was even more reason to cover up. The United States seemed to be standing in the eye of a hurricane of spy cases. Since the announcement of Souther's defection in July 1988, Clyde Lee Conrad, a former army sergeant, had been charged with operating an espionage ring that reported to the Hungarian intelligence service, and Army Warrant Officer James W. Hall III had been sentenced to forty years in prison for revealing extremely sensitive communications intelligence to the Soviets. A month later, the FBI and newspaper reporters began trailing Felix S. Bloch, who had served as deputy chief of mission of the American embassy in Vienna, because of allegations that he was a spy for the Soviet Union. This, coming on top of the cases of John A. Walker, Jr., Ronald W. Pelton, and Edward Lee Howard three years earlier, made one wonder if there were any secrets left to steal.

"The threat against us—despite *perestroika*—has grown," William H. Webster, director of the CIA, told *Newsweek* magazine.[7] He was referring to the increase in spy cases as well as to the obvious need by the U.S. government to remain vigilant at a time when the Soviet Union is undergoing fundamental political changes.

Just after the Souther case broke, Pentagon spokesman Pete Williams told reporters the FBI and NIS had not yet been able to determine what information Souther might have provided to the Soviet Union—or even whether he had spied actively before he defected.[8] It was a flat lie, and following it was a quote from an unnamed senior Defense Department official who called the *Pravda* story "highly unlikely." He said Souther had access to "nothing remotely like" the U.S. Navy's plans in the event of nuclear war.

The truth was that Souther had access to much more than the navy's nuclear war plans. He had access to all of America's nuclear war plans.

While it was clear the Soviets were using Souther's case to rub the noses of American intelligence agencies in their own failures, those familiar with the case had no doubt that Souther gave the Soviets everything they claimed he had—and much more.

What the newspaper stories did not report is that since December 1984, Souther had been assigned to a post so sensitive that its name sounds like a spy novelist's invention. FICEUR-LANT is the Navy's Fleet Intelligence Center for Europe and the Atlantic. Located on the naval base in Norfolk, FICEUR-LANT is housed in a two-story, windowless building. At night, mercury vapor lights bathe its red-brick walls. Ultrasonic, motion detector, and other alarm systems protect it. If an alarm is sounded, more than two dozen marines, armed with M-16 rifles, surround the building.

The security precautions could not be too stringent. The center devises and distributes America's nuclear war plans and receives and processes top-secret spy satellite surveillance photos, National Security Agency communications interceptions, and readings from radar and infrared sensors that go into planning H-bomb delivery routes.

Nor did the newspapers report that since 1982, Souther's

former wife had been trying to report his spy activities to the U.S. government, but with no success.

Finally, the stories gave no hint of the strange pressures that led this young man—who grew up in America's heartland and sang in his church choir—to become a spy.

2

On the windowpanes, gray raindrops
howled together,
piling on a grimace
as though the gargoyles
of Notre Dame were howling.

—VLADIMIR MAYAKOVSKY, "A Cloud
in Trousers"

MUNSTER, INDIANA, where Glenn Michael Souther spent his boyhood, is as far removed from the world of spies as Hollywood is from Washington. A bedroom community forty-two miles southeast of Chicago's O'Hare International Airport, it has neat, small homes with flowers bordering the sidewalks. In the center of town is a tan high school with brown trim. Across the street from the high school is the football field, and behind the school is the public library.

For the immigrant families who populate Chicago, Munster is a refuge, a place to aspire to. Bordered by the rusting, decaying industry of Gary, Calumet City, and Hammond, it is an upper-middle-class suburb where the local doctors and lawyers live. For the few union members who move there, it is a badge of success. The inhabitants of Munster are proud to have arrived, and even prouder that they made it the hard way. For that reason, it is a hard, conservative town, an enclave of twenty-two thousand fiercely patriotic burghers trying to maintain what they have and hand their children something better.

Here Souther (pronounced "suther") spent much of his free time singing in a church choir, attending parties given by a church youth group, and playing the banjo in a band. Souther came across as being fun, personable, and an all-American boy—someone who could be a real charmer with girls, but also, with a beer in his hand as he grew older, one of the guys. With girls, he seemed gentle and caring and sensitive. At other times he was rowdy and fun. He was the type whom everyone loved and who loved everyone.

His physical appearance only enhanced that impression. He had a friendly, trusting face, fresh- and healthy-looking. His hair was combed to the side, with no bangs, no real style. He had the outdoorsy look of one who would love to tackle mountains and who could appreciate the woods, someone who would stop to watch a sunset. His eyes were innocent-looking, with a lost look to them—as if he were searching for something or someone. His easy smile was warm, boyish, and charming.

In a town where eighty percent of the children went on to college, Souther was an above-average student and a member of the cross-country team. He was considered a leader, if a practical joker. At social functions he was the one that made it a party, made it complete. In almost every respect, his was a conventional midwestern upbringing.

Yet there was a crack in this idyllic picture, one that eventually would tear Souther apart. It was an inner torment, a rage as powerful as a tornado, born of his feelings about his father. Later, Souther would identify with the Russian poet Vladimir Mayakovsky, whose life was marked with pain and whose poetic images were frequently raw and brutal. The tortured voice in

Mayakovsky's autobiographical poems cried out in terror of being impaled on spires, trampled by madmen or mobs, consumed by fire, or swept away by storms.[9]

Souther was born just across Interstate 80 from Munster in Hammond, Indiana, on January 30, 1957. It was where Souther's father, Eugene Sherman Souther, had been born and where his grandparents still lived. Souther's father was a businessman, the office manager of the local Wonder Bread bakery. His favorite pastime was golf.

Souther's mother, Shirley Swartz, is a native of Hegwisch, Illinois. She is a secretary who worked at a steel company and a machine company. A year after Glenn was born, the couple had a daughter, Janet, now a hairdresser in Cincinnati. Four years after she was born, they had another son, Timothy, now a mold maker near Rockford, Illinois.[10] Because of money problems, Timothy was sent to live with his mother's parents until he was five.[11]

When Souther was six, his parents divorced. Eugene Souther eventually remarried and moved to Portland, Maine, where he is controller of the Nissen Baking Company; Shirley Souther married Joseph Wiergacz, a labor relations manager whom she met at a steel company where they both worked. She took his name. Since 1978 she had been executive secretary to the president of Loyola Paper Company in Chicago.

Before they were divorced, the Southers lived on Monroe Street in Munster, some five blocks from the Illinois line. The house had three bedrooms and another bedroom in the basement where Glenn slept. He didn't spend time watching television with the rest of the family; he usually kept to himself in his room. Yet he had a number of friends. Souther and several of his friends often appropriated the street for games of baseball or kick-the-can. One time they hit a ball through the next-door neighbor's window. Everyone scattered until James N. Petsas,

one of Glenn's friends, took responsibility. They all agreed to
pay for the damage.

The only departure from a "Father Knows Best" segment
was Souther's habit of wearing a Confederate uniform. Souther
loved to play war games, and he always insisted on playing the
Confederate soldier. Even when going to Eads, the local public
school, he wore a Confederate hat or a Confederate flag on his
jacket.

It was enough of a departure from the routine of life in
Munster for his friends to take notice. Years later, it was one
of the characteristics that most stuck in their minds.

"I remember him dressing as a Confederate soldier," Petsas,
who lived across the street, said. "He wore the Confederate
soldier hat quite a bit, too. He liked that a lot. He just liked to
wear it."[12]

"He wore Confederate uniforms in elementary school," said
James Vitkus, Jr., another friend. "I thought it was strange."[13]

Timothy L. Biter, who lived on the street behind Souther's
house, said Souther loved to wear a Confederate hat even when
they were not playing war games. He recalled that Souther
urged Biter to kiss and undress Janet, Souther's sister. She
seemed to like Biter, but he did not take Souther's advice.

"He said, 'Go over and kiss her,'" Biter said. "I thought,
'That's your sister!'"[14]

In retrospect, Souther's identification with the Confederacy
could be seen as a sign of his resentment of authority and his
attraction to the other side, which he perceived as the underdog.
They were tendencies that would become more pronounced as
he grew older.

In junior high school, Souther became active in the Cove-
nant Presbyterian Church of Hessville, Indiana, which his
mother attended. Clifford E. Duggan, Jr., one of Souther's best
friends at the time, recalled their singing together in the choir,

serving together as camp counselors at a church-run summer camp in Rochester, Indiana, and belonging to Youths for Christ, an evangelical community-service group.

"We went to coffeehouses [and] sat and talked religion," Duggan said. "We were born-again Christians. We would get up and give testimonials. He wasn't baptized again. It was just doing Christian things.[15]

"He was fervently religious," Duggan continued. "It was basic Christian tenets about committing your life to Christ. He went to Bible studies on Wednesday. On Sundays we would go in the morning [to church services] and to an evening service."

Duggan said they both sang in the choir during the evening service. "If you were good enough, you graduated to the morning service," he said.

Usually after the evening service, Souther's group of friends went to a nearby McDonald's. One night, Souther vanished. Around midnight, his mother began calling his friends to find out where he was.

"He ended up having gone to the Pentecostal Church near Hessville Park," said Dave A. Eastwood, whose father was the pastor of the church.[16] "He was riding by and heard them and went in."

In high school, Souther engaged in the usual teenage pranks—draping toilet paper from the branches of trees outside girls' houses or placing blinking caution signs used at construction sites on their front lawns at night. To Souther, there was something magical about the luminescent yellow signs. It was a way of asserting his authority—like a police cruiser coming up behind a driver with an array of flashing lights. Yet the message he conveyed was ambiguous enough so that he could still disavow it. Depending on the girl, a caution sign on her house could be a symbol of distaste or affection. If the girl guessed who had done it, Souther could take refuge in the fact that she could not be sure why he had done it. Thus, if the caution sign was a sign of affection, Souther could not be rejected because the girl did not know the true purpose of the gesture. On the other hand, if it was a symbol of dislike, the girl would never know for sure just why Souther had chosen to bestow a caution sign on her. Usually, the motive was a combination of both emotions—the target might be a girl whom Souther liked but who had rejected him.

Beyond conveying a message, there was something particularly funny about placing a caution sign on a girl's house. When he ran with several friends across a front lawn carrying the ungainly marker, Souther felt like a marine taking a beachhead. He knew that anyone who tried to remove the sign would quickly find that all four legs dropped out as soon as it was lifted. This only added to the bizarre nature of the prank.

Souther also engaged in the typical torture that older siblings visit on their little brothers. Glenn's brother, Tim, kept a stash of *Playboys* in the attic. One day Tim came back from high school and found that Souther had removed the centerfolds and plastered pictures of naked girls all over the outside of a fort that Tim had built in the garage.

"My mom thought I had done it," Tim Souther said.

With his brother, Souther liked to play Risk, a war game played on a map of the world. But one night he asked Tim if he wanted to play penny poker. He threw a deck of cards on the table and left. When Tim looked at them, he was shocked to see that they were pornographic.

When Tim got his first minibike, Souther and a neighborhood friend knocked him off and rode away with it.

The teasing didn't stop as Tim and Souther got older. The

first time Souther talked to Tim's wife on the phone, he said, "So how's your sex life? You guys get it on every night?"

"Holy God, Tim, it's your brother!" she said, quickly handing over the receiver.

One night, Tim and his wife were watching television when the phone rang. Tim answered and heard a sexy female voice saying she would like to kiss intimate parts of his body. Tim blushed as he thought about what he would tell his wife sitting nearby. Then Souther got on the phone.

"Hey, how's it going?" he asked.

Occasionally, Tim would get his revenge. One night back in Munster he came home and found Glenn and several friends skinny-dipping in the backyard pool. He saw a neighbor puttering in his backyard. In a flash, Tim flipped on the rear floodlights. The neighbor looked over at them. Tim could see Souther's eyes meet the neighbor's. Then Souther and his friends ran for cover in the garage.

Both Souther and Duggan had a crush on Mary C. Vance. Known as Missy, she was a very attractive and personable cheerleader with black, shoulder-length hair. It seemed she had everything he would ever want in a girl. But he admired her from afar.

"He may have had a crush on me but we all had a crush on each other back then," she said.[17]

Later, Souther wrote under Vance's photo in her yearbook, "Dear Missy: Ha ha. I was the one that got your house. Tell your parents peace. Good luck, Glenn."

It was a reference to the fact that Souther had toilet-papered—or tee-peed—her house.

It was at a coffeehouse in Lansing, Illinois, right next door to Munster, that Souther met his first love, Amy S. Rodenburg. She was tall and had long brown hair and grayish blue eyes. Souther and Rodenburg had in common their love of Christ.

"We were Jesus freaks," she would later say. "We wore crosses and everything."[18]

Rodenburg was then fourteen; he was fifteen. They would go to church together or meet at the coffeehouse, La Brise. For Christmas, Souther gave her a "Chicago" album. His inscription referred to "Color My World," an optimistic, sentimental tune which they considered their song.

One afternoon in Rodenburg's basement, they began making out.

"We never went all the way, because I didn't want to," she said.

Rodenburg thought the world of Souther. He was handsome, funny, and a nice person, if a bit headstrong. Then, after three months, it was over.

"He seemed disinterested. He hurt me. I always thought what if I met him again? I always remembered he was really funny," she said.

Souther played the banjo in an after-school band that included Duggan, Eastwood, and Dave Glueckert. During the summer, they attended a religious summer camp and played music there as well. Because he was overweight, Glueckert was often the butt of jokes. When the band got a standing ovation one evening, Glueckert began to sob.

"I said, 'What are you doing that for?' It was like everybody had looked at him strangely before. Now he was accepted," said Duggan.[19]

When a cousin of Glueckert's whom they all knew died later that summer of a heart attack, the group attended his funeral.[20] Like Glueckert, the cousin was big and overweight. "He wasn't the fattest kid you ever saw but he was overweight enough so he'd have trouble in sports. He was the kid we all made fun of and called names," said Vance.[21]

Even though Souther was outgoing and popular, he secretly

identified with the overweight boy who died. He saw himself as an underdog, much like the dead boy. It underlined the difference between his image of himself and the way others saw him. He would later attribute some of his behavior to the way he saw the young man being treated.

3

AFTER HIS DIVORCE, Souther's father visited his three children every other Sunday. He would pick them up after church and drive them to his parents' home in Hammond, where the children would play in the backyard.

Tim Souther felt his father favored Glenn over him and Janet. Yet even with Glenn, his father came across as cold, imperious, and tight with money, according to Tim. So far as Tim knew, that was one reason for his parents' divorce.

"I know my dad was real selfish," Tim Souther would say later. "He wouldn't let my mom spend any money for the house. Otherwise she didn't say much about it [the divorce] that I know. Just that he was real stingy. She bought a lamp for the house and he had a fit."[22]

After the divorce, Tim Souther came to realize that his father was as cold as dry ice.

"He was never there when I needed him," Tim Souther

said. To this day, he said, his father has not seen his grand-children.

"I have two kids, a four- and a five-year-old," he said. "At Christmas, he was out here [near Chicago] and called me up. The last time I had heard from him was two Christmases ago. He called me and asked if I wanted to come out and see him . . . in Chicago. The kids were kind of sick. It would be taking a chance to take them in the car out to Chicago. I asked if he could come here. He said he had just flown in and his in-laws' tires were pretty bad. I said it's thirty-five minutes away. But [I later learned] he went two hours to see a friend in Indiana. Right away that tells you something. He hadn't seen my kids at all at that point, and still hasn't. I don't even think of him as being my dad. I don't know why he's like that."[23]

Tim Souther said that during another visit to Chicago, "My father wanted to have dinner with me. He called out here and said he would pick me up. He said, 'Ask your sister. Girls need more time to get ready.' She said it would take forty-five minutes. I called him and he said never mind. He can't wait forty-five minutes. I called her and told her. She got mad at me. Now she won't talk to him. He's never been there for me. He wants me to come to him.

"He would only show his face on occasions like Christmas when he knew he had to. Otherwise, he was not around," Tim said, adding that his father treated Glenn in much the same way.

Unlike Tim and Janet, Souther stayed out late, took risks, and constantly became involved in pranks—a pattern that continued even as he grew older. For his new stepfather, Glenn was a handful. And somehow Glenn always managed to shift the blame to Tim.

One day Wiergacz, Souther's stepfather, noticed their red Volkswagen had dents in the roof. Glenn blamed Tim, even though he had dented the car when he drove it into a snowbank after one of Chicago's heaviest snowfalls.

On a few occasions Wiergacz lost his temper and hit Tim. Once, he apparently hit Glenn.[24] Tim never held a grudge but Glenn couldn't forget. Later, when he was an adult, Glenn would bring it up and say he would never forgive his stepfather.

Souther spent much of his time locked in his room in the basement of the house in Munster. He would tell his mother he was listening to stereo music through headphones. Because it was so difficult to get through to him, she had a buzzer installed so she could call him for dinner by pushing a button upstairs.

But Souther was doing more than listening to music. As he would later confide to a girlfriend, he had a compulsive need to masturbate. The compulsion was so abnormal that he raised painful lesions on his penis. While doing research for a psychology paper, she read about the problem in the American Psychiatric Association's *Diagnostic and Statistical Manual of Mental Disorders*. She decided that Souther suffered from an obsessive compulsive disorder.[25]

4

But night oozed and oozed through the room—
and the eye, weighed down, could not slither out of the slime.

—VLADIMIR MAYAKOVSKY, "A Cloud in Trousers"

WHEN Souther was in his junior year in high school, his father persuaded him to move to Maine and live with him. Glenn never explained to his brother his reasons for leaving, but he told a friend it was an easy out for him because of his resentment of his stepfather.[26]

Souther's father lives in Cumberland, a town of quiet residential streets a half hour north of Portland on the coast of Maine. Cumberland is divided into Cumberland Center, the main part of town; West Cumberland, which is more inland; and Cumberland Foreside, where Glenn's father lives. Cumberland Center is a suburban area, an enclave of the middle class. Cumberland West is more blue-collar. Cumberland Foreside, near the water, is the wealthy section.

Souther's father lives with his wife, Marilyn, in a rustic wood-frame colonial house on Heritage Lane, a quiet street just off Route 88. The house is typically Maine—freshly painted white shutters against weathering brown shingles and a bay window draped with ruffled curtains. A Robert Frost rock wall separates the manicured lawn from the wild, wooded lot next door. The landscaping is sparse; beyond the Cadillac parked outside, the deck in back is the house's only sign of affluence.

The home is a mile from the town landing on an inlet of Casco Bay, a parking spot for the local teenagers. But more important, in Souther's case, there is water everywhere, and the call of the sea.

Souther entered Greely High School in Cumberland in the second semester of his junior year. From the first day in January 1973 when he began school there, Souther was one of the most popular students in his class. He was outgoing and had a sense of humor. Moreover, he had a way of engaging in outrageous activities without offending anyone.

Rebecca Bendixon, a sandy-haired girl who dated Souther during his senior year, recalled that they had an English teacher who was nine months pregnant.

"He would chase her all over the room. He said, 'You better sit down! You better sit down!' He was the only one who could have gotten away with that."[27]

Several girls became offended because Souther would date them briefly and then drop them, a pattern Souther would repeat throughout his life. The girls in Maine attributed it to his Chicago background.

"Basically, relationships were one-on-one," said Joyce Cleveland, a friend of Souther's from high school. "A lot of the girls felt they were not good enough and felt hurt that they didn't get access to him. He was dating a lot of different girls and dropped them and went on to someone else. A lot of them got together and compared notes. He came from a different area where casual dating was the only way you dated in high school. It took them awhile to understand that."[28]

In Cumberland, said Cleveland, "There was nothing to do. You had to have access to a car and go into Portland. Most of us did not and mostly you would go out with one person; you'd go over to their house and watch TV, or they'd come over to yours. Occasionally we'd go to the gravel pit and have a party."

The gravel pit, in nearby North Yarmouth, was a depression in a sand and gravel deposit.

"They [the owners] let them do it because otherwise we'd be driving around. After a couple of hours the old man would come down and say, 'Okay, folks, time to go.' If they didn't leave, he'd call the cops in," Cleveland said.

"Glenn was smart in class. He studied but not a lot. He would know the material if he read it over. He would participate in class and know the answers. He would not be in the back of the class or in the front. He wasn't teacher's pet. He always gave his opinion. He debated with you. But he wasn't pushy. We didn't have a lot of political attitudes back then. It was the 'me' generation, nothing to rally behind. It was very apolitical."

Like Souther, Cleveland had a small part in the senior play, *Up the Down Staircase*. Souther enjoyed acting and did it well. As a memento, Souther, Cleveland, and several others stuffed a beer bottle down the tank behind a toilet backstage. Inside, they stuffed a note referring to their class. The bottle stuck in the toilet like a time capsule.

Souther loved to ride his ten-speed bike through town, and there was a widespread rumor that he had gotten a speeding ticket for his bicycle riding. "The Cumberland police would come in the parking lot at the high school, and pull you over looking for taillights out," Cleveland said. "Then sometimes they would follow you all the way home, just trying to catch you doing something. I believe they only gave him a warning. I don't believe they gave him a ticket."[29]

Souther's best friend at Greely was Robert A. Fitch, a soft-spoken, slightly built runner with fine hands, dark brown eyes, and a very finely chiseled face. They shared an interest in sports and religion. They often discussed Christ and his grace in dying and providing salvation for man.

"He [Souther] was interested in track. I ran track," Fitch recalled. "He was interested in biking, and I was into biking. In track season, we'd train together. He was a distance runner and I was a sprinter. We'd run together and spend time driving around, going to soccer games, and spending time at his house," he said.[30] "If we saw a car full of girls, we'd follow them around."

One weekend Souther decided he wanted to go hiking on Mount Katahdin, the tallest mountain in Maine. It was winter and he hadn't done much hiking.

"He bought boots and equipment and tried to recruit others," Fitch said. "I didn't want to go. I suppose part of it was I felt it was foolhardy. He tried to recruit a couple of others who backed out. So he went by himself. His parents didn't know what he was up to. Apparently he smooth-talked the rangers into letting him go in, claiming he had experience."

Souther fell through a snow bridge into a freezing stream. When he failed to come down from the mountain, the rangers looked for him and brought him out.

"He showed up on Sunday at church and wanted me to go to his folks' house with him. He thought his dad would not get as angry with someone else around," Fitch said.

As in any high school, everyone wondered who was having sex. The general belief was that no one was. In Souther's case, that was right.

After school Souther worked for the thrift store run by the

Nissen Baking Company, where his father was an executive. The thrift store sold bakery products whose pull dates had expired.

"We were going to have a senior breakfast, and we needed pastries, so Glenn went in with a pickup truck and really loaded it up. He kind of helped himself. That didn't go over too well," Fitch said.

Fitch double-dated with Souther to the senior prom. They had reservations for dinner at the Sheraton near the airport at 7:15 P.M.

"The place was packed. We were in tuxedos and had to wait quite a while in the lounge. Finally Glenn talked to the maître d'," Fitch said. "Apparently he was waiting for someone to slip him some money. Glenn was really hot under the collar. Finally we got out of there at ten-fifteen and got to the prom at a quarter to eleven. We told Glenn's dad, and he called them up, and they offered to give us a free dinner."

Fitch said Souther, to get even, took some silverware when he left the restaurant.[31]

Souther graduated in June 1975. His yearbook entry included the usual array of phrases and quotations referring to events that were important then but are now long forgotten.

Despite their closeness during high school, Souther and Fitch had begun to drift apart by graduation. Fitch was a born-again Christian. While Souther was interested in religion when he had first moved from Chicago, it seemed to Fitch that he had become more involved with drinking and going to parties by the end of high school.

Given the closeness of their friendship, Souther's yearbook inscription to his friend Fitch was chilly. "Bob, I had a good time here, especially this year with the play and all," Souther wrote under Fitch's photo. "I did such a good job, you too. Just kidding. Have fun in college."

By graduation time, Souther's problems with his father had become more noticeable.

"I got the feeling he didn't have a happy home life," said Kimerly Caine, who went to the senior prom with him, largely, she explained, because no one else asked her. "He didn't like his father much. They had a real personality conflict. His father had a lot of money and didn't share it with Glenn. I didn't think they had much contact."[32]

Tim Souther also said Souther told him he was having problems with his father.

"He was eighteen and had a curfew of nine-thirty or ten with my dad," Tim Souther said. But things had been different when he lived with his mother. "We never even had curfews when we were young."

Eventually, Souther and his father came into conflict over Souther's future plans. Souther's father wanted him to go to college. Souther wanted to go into the service and become a photographer. It was a typical clash of late adolescence, except that Souther's father even wanted to choose the college.

"He would pay for Glenn's college, but he had to go to the one he chose and take the courses he chose, or he couldn't go," Tim Souther said. "He said he [their father] was a jerk."[33]

"I think he felt his father expected too much from him and wouldn't let him live his life," Fitch said. "They had a parting of the ways. He resented him. I know he told me his father had certain plans for him, and Glenn had things he wanted to do. Going to college may have been part of it. His dad felt instead of going into the service he would have been better off getting a college education. Glenn wanted to get into photography. His father wasn't big on that."

But the resentment went further than that.

"It was more that Glenn was a free spirit and his goals were not to be v.p. of a bakery and settle into an upper-middle-class background," Fitch said. "Glenn's approach was to have an idea and follow it. He resented his dad's efforts to fit him into a mold.[34]

"His father is very stern, businesslike," Fitch added. It seemed to Glenn he was always scowling.[35]

Because of pressure from his father, Souther agreed to go to Purdue University/Calumet in Hammond, Indiana. He lived with his mother and stepfather and spent much of his time taking photos for the school paper. One time, according to what he told his brother, Tim, he stole some books from the library by sneaking into the freight elevator at night. By the end of the first semester, he had dropped out. He enlisted in the navy on January 4, 1976.

Soon he would find a way to act out his feelings about his father.

5

You swept in abruptly
like "take it or leave it!"
Mauling your suede gloves,
you declared:
"D'you know,
I'm getting married."

—VLADIMIR MAYAKOVSKY, "A Cloud
    in Trousers"

S O U T H E R entered boot camp at Great Lakes, Illinois, and was
sent to Pensacola, Florida, to attend photography school. He
later told friends from Maine that he loved the discipline of the
navy.

"When they asked him to do push-ups, he said, 'Yes, sir,'"
his friend Bob Fitch said.

After finishing school in June 1976, Souther was assigned
to the nuclear-powered aircraft carrier U.S.S. *Nimitz* as a petty
officer. With a security clearance of secret, he flew in navy
planes to take photos of Soviet ships. In addition, he developed
his own and others' photographs. Later, he was a photo lab
supervisor and prepared briefing materials for the commander.
After marrying an Italian woman and becoming fluent in her
language, Souther occasionally served as an interpreter, too.

Despite worsening relations with his father, he sent him
several enlargements of Soviet planes. His father had always

been interested in military airplanes. The photos were classified. Souther already was flouting the security rules.

When Souther returned home for Christmas on leave, he showed the photos to his friend Bob Fitch. Even though the photos had no classification markings, Souther told Fitch they were classified.[36]

"I remember one picture he showed me," Fitch said. "It was a Russian bomber taken from the air from another plane."

Souther showed the pictures to Fitch in a matter-of-fact way. He seemed neither proud that he had them nor furtive about the fact that they were classified. But Fitch was impressed that Souther had "little regard for the rules."

During the same visit back home, Souther saw Rebecca Bendixon, his high school girlfriend. It was then that they first had sex.

"The first time was when he came back on leave," she said. "In high school, it was making out."[37]

By then, Souther was experienced. Based on what he told others, he already had had sex with several women in Italy.

That summer, Souther met Patrizia Di Palma on the isle of Capri, a stately jewel nestled in the Bay of Naples. Souther always attracted the most gorgeous women, and Di Palma was no exception. With wide-set green eyes as big as half dollars, she had frosted light brown hair, high cheekbones, and a model's build.

Growing up in Naples, near the U.S. Navy's Sixth Fleet home port of Gaeta, Di Palma had met many navy men and had no use for them. She considered them coarse and stupid. Glenn was different. He was sensitive, bright, and intellectually stimulating, if a bit brash. Moreover, she liked his slim build, sparkling hazel eyes, and luxuriant brown beard.

Although not wealthy, Di Palma's family was descended from Italian nobles. Di Palma had attended college in Naples and worked at part-time jobs. Then nineteen, she was vacationing on Capri with friends when she met Souther in 1976. He was taking pictures in a square. Souther was attracted to her statuesque shape in a bathing suit, her green eyes, her clear skin, and her easy laugh.

Souther took pictures of her, and she gave him her address so he could mail copies to her. At the time, she did not understand English, so they communicated in improvised sign language.[38]

Soon they were dating, and after a month Souther proposed. Di Palma thought he must be crazy and decided to stop seeing him. However, after the *Nimitz* returned to the States, Souther regularly wrote to her. The relationship became more serious, and when the aircraft carrier returned to Gaeta, about an hour-and-a-half drive north of Naples, she agreed to see him again. On April 23, 1978, they were married.

Di Palma was not religious, but to please her parents she and Souther married in a Catholic church in Rome. Di Palma recalled that when he came to the wedding, Souther's father played the role of "the ugly American."

"He didn't like anything [in Italy]," she said. "He was so stupid. He would look at the buildings and say the people live in those places? Yecch! The cars were too small. Everything he didn't like."[39]

Later, Souther would tell Di Palma that his father had a closed mind, and that Souther resented what he had done to his mother. He said his father did not care about his kids and had no relationship with Souther's brother and sister.[40] On the other hand, Souther embraced Di Palma's family as his own.

"At last I've found a close family," he told her, referring to her parents.

In February 1979, Souther left the *Nimitz* and was assigned to "B" school at Pensacola, Florida, for more specialized training in photography for intelligence purposes. In April he was assigned to the U.S.S. *Albany* and later the U.S.S. *Puget Sound* in Gaeta. As the successive flagships for the U.S. Navy's Sixth Fleet, the ships served as headquarters for the commander of the fleet. They were loaded with classified intelligence, and this gave Souther access for the first time to highly sensitive information.

It was while based on these ships that Souther developed an interest in Communism, substituting for the equally strong religious beliefs which he previously held. How that happened may never be known. However, it is clear he was becoming more resentful of the navy and the authority it represented. Although he impressed all his superiors, he had a new boss whom he hated. He told Di Palma that the man liked to show his power by requiring underlings to clean the toilets with a toothbrush. At the same time, his marriage began to deteriorate, and his interest in Communism became one of the many points of contention.

Di Palma first noticed a change when he began reading books about Trotsky and Lenin. "Why are you reading about Communism?" she would ask him. "It could be dangerous in your position."[41]

"I'm just curious," he said.

"I think the basic theory of Communism is good. Everybody is the same, there are no different classes," Di Palma told Souther. "But this is unrealistic."

As time went on, Souther become more open about his feelings. He insisted the Communist model would work. He described the United States as a materialistic and imperialistic nation.

"Americans are all ignorant," Souther told her. "They care only about their own country. In Europe everything is different."

"I'm sure the U.S. is imperialistic," Di Palma would say.

34

"They are everywhere in the world. But the Soviets are, too—Hungary, Czechoslovakia, Afghanistan, Cuba." The big difference, she said, is that in the Communist countries, "They are not free."

Di Palma spoke from personal experience. Since the unemployment rate in the south of Italy is nearly one-third, she had briefly thought of teaching Italian to Bulgarians as a career. During a visit to Bulgaria in 1977, she met some Soviet journalists who got drunk and told her how their articles were censored. She was shocked to find that restaurants there had no milk or fruit. She had to stand in line for hours to buy milk in a store.

Souther and Di Palma both wanted to have a baby, and when their son, Angelo, was born on September 21, 1981, Souther insisted on being at the birth, which was by cesarean section. He took photographs that he would later hang on his wall. One of the pictures won a photography contest.

"He has to become an important person and not become like me," Souther said of the baby.

It was but another facet of his contradictory character. Even though he was gregarious and perceived as a leader, he thought of himself as an underdog and a loner. Even though he was advancing in the navy and had married a gorgeous woman, he saw himself as unimportant. It was but another facet of the split between his image of himself and reality.

When the baby was born, Souther excitedly called his mother to tell her the good news. Souther's father never accepted Di Palma because she was not an American. In phone conversations, he insisted on calling Angelo "Steve"—short for his middle name of Stephan.[42]

"Who is Steve?" Di Palma would say when Souther's father asked about the baby.

Souther played with Angelo and seemed to enjoy being a

father. Yet he had started drinking excessively and was erratic. Souther had taught Di Palma to play the war game Risk in English. Her English had improved so much that she routinely beat him at it. He would become furious, and one day he threw the game away.

Moreover, Souther was becoming paranoid, or so it seemed to his wife. One afternoon the buzzer in their apartment rang from downstairs.

"*Pulizia*," a woman said over the intercom.

"Police? What do they want? Why are they here?" Souther asked.[43] Clearly, he was frightened.

Di Palma picked up the receiver.

"*Pulizia*," the woman said again.

Di Palma realized what had happened. Souther had mistaken the Italian word for cleaning people—*pulizia*—for *polizia*, which means police.

Di Palma didn't like to cook, so they would go to restaurants with friends. One day just before the baby was born she went to the U.S.S. *Puget Sound* to tell Souther about a social engagement she had made for them. He wasn't there. She was told that Souther had the day off. Di Palma started to think he was seeing another woman.

In fact, several friends later told her that he was seeing an attractive fellow navy photographer based on the ship. But it turned out he was doing more than dallying with women.

It was during one of Souther's drinking binges, while they were arguing about the many mundane things they argued about, that he told Di Palma he was working for the Soviets.

"One day I went to the Soviet embassy in Rome and told them that I wanted to work for them. Not for money but because I believed in Communism," Souther told her in the fall of 1981. He said he had gone to the embassy the year before —1980—and had been working for the Soviets ever since. He

36

also said he had a Soviet passport. He mentioned that others were spying on the ship, as if that would make it all right.[44]

At first Di Palma thought he was making up stories. He was drunk when he told her. His point seemed to be that he had more important things to worry about than their marital harmony. But more and more, Souther was engaged in reading books about Communism, and as she became more aware of his bizarre activities, she came to realize he was a spy.

Souther bought a shortwave radio, telling Di Palma that he thought it would be fun to listen to foreign broadcasts. But one night Di Palma saw him listening to it at 1:00 A.M. She watched him from a doorway, and his back was to her, so he didn't see her. Souther was listening to sets of numbers that were being broadcast in English in monotonous tones. Each group of numbers consisted of five digits. As he heard the numbers, Souther wrote them down in a notebook. Then he removed a pen from a canvas bag he always carried. He opened the pen and took out thin white paper rolled up inside. He wrote on the paper, rolled it up, and replaced it in the pen.

As she lay awake that night, Di Palma kept turning this new information over in her mind. She had heard enough about spying from books and movies to realize Souther was using some sort of code. She wondered what kind of information her husband was giving the Soviets. She thought about the fact that her husband had been expressing increasing resentment about his new boss. He was a mean son of a bitch. But was that any reason to spy against his own country? Most of all, she worried that he would get caught. But a few days later, Souther reassured her.

"To do what I'm doing, I have to be perfect at work so they won't be suspicious. To throw off suspicion, I'm a model sailor," he boasted.

Indeed, in March 1981, Souther received a letter of com-

----

mendation from the commander of the Sixth Fleet for outstanding performance of his duties. In October 1981 he
received the Outstanding Sailor of the Quarter award of the
Sixth Fleet.

Just after she saw him use the shortwave radio, Di Palma
and Souther drove from Gaeta to Naples for the weekend.
Souther always drove fast. Di Palma would ask him to drive
slower. He would ignore her, and they often argued about it.
One time when Di Palma asked him to slow down he got so
mad that he broke the rearview mirror with his fist and cut his
hand. Driving from Gaeta to Naples, Souther was going even
faster than usual.

"What's the rush?" Di Palma asked him.

"I'm late," Souther answered.

"Late for what?" she asked.

"I have to make a very important call," he said.

"What kind of call?" Di Palma asked.

Souther became mad.

"It's none of your business," he said.

"If you don't want to tell me something, don't say anything,"
she said.

They went to a pay phone and Souther placed the call.
Looking over his shoulder, Di Palma was able to see the number
he dialed. She memorized it. After he said a few words into the
receiver, Souther told Di Palma, "Everything is okay."

Later, Di Palma dialed the number. A bowling alley answered. Di Palma hung up.

Di Palma never saw any money from the Soviets. But after
Angelo was born, Souther mentioned that "they" had given him
cash as a gift when their son was born. By then, Di Palma knew
that when Souther referred to "them," he meant the Soviets.

Di Palma decided the tan canvas bag Souther always carried

must contain secrets he was hiding. Souther took it with him to work, when they went to restaurants, and even to parties. Once she asked him what it contained.

"It's none of your business," he snarled at her. "Stay out of my life. Stay out of my things." Then he added menacingly, "I would kill my son for the right cause."

One afternoon when Souther had gone to do an errand, Di Palma noticed that he had left the bag in their bedroom. Furtively, she unzipped the top and looked inside. It contained maps of the area where they lived and rolls of film. On the maps, different locations were circled. In addition, Di Palma found a picture of an American officer with his wife. She also found the notebook Souther had used for writing the coded messages he took down over his shortwave radio. Finally, she found an Olympus camera with a special lens. Since she was interested in photography herself, she knew something about lenses. She had never seen one like this. Moreover, it had no brand name on it.

Later, Di Palma asked at a camera store if the Olympus had such a lens as an accessory.

"The lens doesn't exist," the man told her.

Di Palma's mind was spinning. She decided the lens must have been made especially for him. It must have something to do with photographing documents. By now she had come to understand that her husband was a spy. Perhaps the Soviets gave him the camera, she thought. Still, Di Palma forced herself not to think about it. For an Italian family, divorce was a disgrace. She was confused and unhappy but not ready to leave him.[45]

Souther was due to be transferred to the Naval Air Training Command at Patuxent River, Maryland. He was mad because he wanted either to become an officer or to leave the navy by the end of the year. He did not see why he should have to transfer back to the United States for the remaining nine months. After Souther came back from a trip to Greece, he told Di Palma their marriage was over. He did not want to take her to the States.

"I have to be alone," Souther said. "We got married too early, and I'm not doing what I wanted to do. I don't love you anymore or want you anymore. I'm tired of being married."[46]

He dropped her almost as abruptly as he had dropped his junior high school sweetheart, Amy Rodenburg.

That night Souther went out and did not return. Sobbing, Di Palma called an NIS agent to report him missing. The NIS agent told her that he had seen Souther lately with the navy photographer Di Palma had heard he was seeing. When he returned the next day, Di Palma accused Souther of seeing another woman, but he said they were just friends.

Souther would later tell his brother and his friends that the cause of their breakup was an affair Di Palma had had with a friend of Souther's from the navy. Souther had trusted him enough to give his friend the key to their house. The man had reciprocated by using the key to come to the house and seduce his wife. He told Di Palma that her husband did not care about her.

"He told me he loved me, that my husband treats me like dirt, that he went out with all the girls wherever he went," she said. "I was pregnant. He wanted me to go with him. I said I loved my husband. I wanted to stay with him. Then one day my husband said some people on the ship said the baby was not his, it was [his friend's]. He told me he didn't believe me. When [the friend] had come to the house, I was already pregnant. I got so disgusted with everything. He said, 'If I see [him], I'll kill him.' "[47]

A few days after telling Di Palma their marriage was over, Souther called his mother in Chicago. He was drunk. He told her he didn't want to see *her* anymore either.

"Forget my number, forget you have a son. I'm tired of America and Americans," he said.

6

You're teasing me now?
"You have fewer emeralds of madness
than a beggar has kopecks!"
But remember!
When they teased Vesuvius,
Pompeii perished!

—VLADIMIR MAYAKOVSKY, "A Cloud
   in Trousers"

ON FEBRUARY 16, 1982, Souther attained the rank of photographer's mate first class. In April he was assigned to Patuxent River, where he took photos of new navy weapons systems and planes. Di Palma begged Souther to take her with him.

"I don't want to live without you," she said.

Souther relented and agreed to take her to the States.

Now Di Palma thought their troubles were behind them. Souther told her he loved her. But their marriage continued to crumble as she found new evidence of his other life.

One day Souther left his wallet at home when he went to work. Curious, Di Palma looked through it and found a key for a rented U.S. Postal Service box. Then she found a receipt for the rental of the box. Di Palma went to the main post office at the Patuxent River naval air station. The numbers on the boxes there didn't match the one on the receipt. She drove to another post office and found the box. She opened it; it was empty.

Di Palma took the receipt to a clerk and said she had lost the key and needed another. She paid a dollar and got her own key to Souther's mailbox.

"When does the mail usually arrive?" she asked the clerk.

"About ten-thirty in the morning," he said.

For the next several weeks, Di Palma checked the box every morning, trying to get there before Souther did. No mail ever came.

Usually Di Palma had no car. Souther left her alone in their rented home in the woods while he went to work in their red Renault with a white stripe. She was becoming increasingly frustrated with her lot. One day, in the heat of an argument, she implied she might tell on Souther.

"If you say anything, I'll kill you, Angelo, and all your family," he said.[48]

On another occasion, Di Palma asked Souther, "Why don't you stop it [spying]?"

"I wish I could stop, but I can't. They won't let me," he said.[49] Then he started crying.

Occasionally, Souther took his wife to parties given by navy colleagues. It was through these contacts that she met coworkers who dropped hints that Souther was seeing yet another navy photographer, Kelli Templeton.

Templeton was fun-loving and got along well with women and men. She stood nearly six feet tall and had long, sexy hair, brown with red highlights. She had no bangs; her hair was all one length and parted in the middle. It was the kind of hairstyle that a flower child from the seventies might have, but her wavy hair had spring. She curled it behind her ears. Most of the time she wore round glasses like a librarian's, brown-rimmed to match her hair. Her eyes were blue and clear, with thin dark

---

eyebrows sketched above them lined by dark eyelashes. Her nose was pugged and cute. She had a long wide mouth and a big friendly smile which flashed teeth worthy of a Crest commercial. She had fair skin, milky and blemishless. She had a shapely body that men never failed to notice.

When she first met her, Di Palma had liked her. Then one day Di Palma listened in on another phone as Souther called Templeton at the photo lab. She heard them make plans to see each other. When Di Palma asked Souther what he was doing, he made up a story.

Di Palma discussed her suspicions with a friend from the photo lab.

"You know, you're right, because many times we can't find them and they're locked in a darkroom together," the friend said.[50]

Di Palma confronted Templeton and demanded that she leave Souther alone.

"I like your husband, but we're not fooling around. We're friends," Templeton said.[51]

One afternoon Di Palma visited the photo lab where Souther and Templeton both worked. She asked where Souther was. At first, she was told no one knew. But somebody found Souther. She suspected he had been in a darkroom with Kelli.

That night Di Palma became hysterical and told Souther she was going to "go walking"—she didn't know or care where. She wanted to test how much he cared about her.

"Okay," he said.

Crying, she went stumbling down a deserted road. The local police picked her up and brought her home.

A few days later Souther arranged for a friend of his to take Di Palma to a discotheque. Di Palma thought it might be so Souther could see Templeton at home or talk to her without any interference. When they got home, Souther told the friend

44

that Di Palma was a bad person because she had gone out without him—even though he'd set it up in the first place.

That weekend, several people from the photo lab invited Souther, Di Palma, and their baby for dinner. Templeton was among the guests. As Souther continued drinking and the hour got late, Di Palma said they would have to go home because she had to put Angelo to sleep.

Souther was livid. He took Di Palma home and then beat her, kicking her in the face. Di Palma was covered with bruises, and her lips were split.

Souther then called the people who had invited them to dinner and invited everyone still at the party to his house. When the other photographers saw Di Palma, they were shocked.

"Don't make that face. Let's have fun!" Souther said to them.

Drunkenly, Souther ran off into the woods with Templeton. Di Palma imagined them having sex together and decided he just wanted to hurt her.[52] She thought of going to the police. But the next day Souther looked at Di Palma and said, "I can't believe that I did that."

It was a typical gesture. A brilliant manipulator, Souther would alternate between begging Di Palma to leave him and calling her a "wonderful wife."

The following day, Souther told Di Palma, "I need time. I need to be alone." He asked Di Palma to stay with his mother in Chicago for a week.

Di Palma decided to leave him alone as he had requested because she understood he had problems. Souther's mother, Shirley Wiergacz, treated Di Palma like a daughter. For a month, Di Palma called Souther every day. It seemed he would never ask her to come back. Finally, Di Palma decided to come back anyway. At the age of twenty-four she had not yet developed enough sense of her own identity to feel capable of living apart from him. Moreover, she had a small baby to support, and his personal magnetism always swept away any doubts she had about the wisdom of remaining with him.

Di Palma asked him to meet her at the airport. When he was not there, she took a taxi. The next day he took her back to the airport to return her to Chicago. Shortly after that, in May 1982, Di Palma and her son left for Italy.

They would never see him again.

7

I feel
my "I"
is much too small for me.
Stubbornly a body pushes out of me.

—VLADIMIR MAYAKOVSKY, "A Cloud
in Trousers"

TO GET HER to leave, Souther promised Di Palma that if she returned to Italy, he would eventually meet her there and bring her back to the States. He claimed he would come over before September 21, 1982, Angelo's birthday. When September came and he did not show up, Di Palma called her husband at Patuxent River and said she would meet him there.

"I don't want you to come," he told her.

Di Palma became hysterical. Her father, a retired engineer-draftsman, took the phone and told Souther, "I'm going to kill you."[53]

Two days after Angelo's birthday, one of Di Palma's brothers-in-law was walking past a restaurant in Rome. Through the window he saw Souther. The navy man was sitting alone at a table. He appeared to be waiting for someone.

"What are you doing here?" the brother-in-law asked him.

"I'm going to go to Naples tomorrow," Souther said.

47

The next day, Souther called Di Palma. "I'm not coming because I'm in the States," he said.

But her brother-in-law had told her he'd spotted Souther, and she rushed to Rome to try to find him. Since hotels in Europe must report to the police the names of any foreigners staying overnight, she thought it would be easy to track him down. After a week of trying, she gave up. Souther was staying with someone else, had used a phony passport when registering, or had left.

Meanwhile, Di Palma had found that there was only enough money in their joint bank account to write a few checks. Besides their car, which Souther kept, they had no other assets.

At first, Di Palma tried to convince herself that he was trying to protect his family from his spying activities. Then she decided he was simply a selfish person. When they were married, he had seemed so sensitive and thoughtful. She wondered if he was acting then or acting now.

"I can't believe a person can forget his own son. It's something my mind can't understand. He left me with nothing," she would later say.

But then, like a pendulum, she would swing from despising him to longing for him. She felt no one would ever replace him. He was her first real love, the father of her baby, someone she had always admired. It was inconceivable to her that all they had shared together could mean nothing, that he could toss her off like a wet bathing suit, treat her as a stranger. If that was the case, life did not seem worth living, she thought to herself.

As she contemplated her predicament, Di Palma debated whether she should report him to the Naval Investigative Service. Normally, the FBI investigates espionage. However, when the suspect is in the military, the military investigative agencies have jurisdiction.

On December 31, 1982, Di Palma was attending a New Year's Eve party in Gaeta, the Italian port where Souther had been assigned. Gaeta is a picturebook town of houses painted pink and orange perched on hillsides, villas built into the earth like ancient temples, rocky hills dropping down to a calm inlet of sea, and great ships in anchor that stand out boldly against the dark water.

By now, Souther was back in the States, but one of Di Palma's sisters was married to a navy officer. Realizing she was depressed about the breakup of her marriage, he invited Di Palma to the party at the home of a fellow officer. But Di Palma had more important things on her mind.

Di Palma was bitter. Her husband had left her penniless with a two-year-old son to support. She felt no obligation to protect him. Indeed, she wanted revenge. Yet in some ways she still loved him. When she spotted a Naval Investigative Service agent whom she had met before, all the anger came to the surface.

"I have to talk with you about my husband," she said.

It was just before midnight, and Gregory A. Scovel, like most of the others at the party, had been drinking. An overweight blond man, he was one of two NIS agents assigned to the NIS office in Gaeta. His job was to investigate criminal allegations against members of the navy. He had been an NIS agent two years and had no experience in counterintelligence, the business of catching spies.

"Would you mind stepping into the bathroom?" Di Palma said to him.

Scovel was taken aback. After all, his wife was at the party. What would she think if she saw him stepping into the bathroom with this fetching young woman?

Di Palma's hair was layered and styled upward, youthfully, and brushed away from her face. She had dark expressive eyebrows, arched like wings above her almond-shaped eyes. Her eyes were gentle and caring, like the eyes of your mother, best friend, or someone you don't mind sharing your feelings with and opening up to. She had apple cheeks, soft and touchable and round, like a toddler's. Her nose, like her other features, was straight and round. Her mouth curled into a vague but sweet smile. Her lips were tight-looking. The corners of her mouth were sharp and precise. She wore stylish clothes.

That evening she had had a few glasses of wine. Alcohol always made her sleepy, and she had never gotten drunk in her life.

Despite his misgivings, Scovel agreed to meet Di Palma in the first-floor bathroom. She was already there when he walked in. She closed the door and faced him.

"I think my husband is working for the Soviets," Di Palma said.

Scovel thought about his wife. He wanted to go back to the party. He felt uncomfortable talking with an attractive woman in the bathroom. It was unseemly. And he was off duty. Espionage was a serious subject that should be discussed in an office, preferably from behind a desk. Besides, he had terrorist threats to worry about just then, not spies.

Scovel did not ask Di Palma any questions.

"I'll call you in ten days to talk about it," he said.[54]

Di Palma felt relieved. She had gotten it off her chest. Now she waited for Scovel to call.

Two days later, Di Palma heard from her brother-in-law, Jeffrey Smallwood, who was married to one of her two sisters. Smallwood was then a lieutenant in the navy. He had been one of Souther's superiors on the *Puget Sound*.

Smallwood was angry. He said that the day after the New Year's Eve party, Scovel had told him of Di Palma's allegation and asked his opinion.

50

"It's absurd," Smallwood said he told the NIS agent. "I know they're having marital problems. I think they're getting a divorce. She's obviously just saying this to get him into trouble."[55]

"But it's true," Di Palma said of her allegation.

"I don't want to hear anything about it. I don't want to be involved. You're just upset with your husband. That's why you want to give him problems," Smallwood said. He said Scovel told him he thought she was crazy, too.[56]

Scovel never did call Di Palma. The NIS agent would later tell his superiors that he saw Di Palma a month later out on the street. Allegedly, he asked her, "Is there anything you want to talk about? Do you have any problems?"

He claimed she answered in the negative.[57]

But Di Palma recalls no such meeting. She does recall seeing Scovel a year later in Gaeta. However, he asked no questions about Souther, she says. In any case, she felt that Scovel's attitude toward her was condescending and insulting. He obviously considered her a nonentity. In view of the way he had brushed her off, she had no intention of telling him anything.

"He didn't want to listen to me," she said. "What problems can I have? What should I tell him? He said he was going to call and he didn't. Then he asks me if I have problems! [The NIS] treated me like a stupid person—as if I just wanted to have revenge," she said.[58]

What is clear is that Scovel took no action on Di Palma's allegation. He did not ask her why she thought her husband was a spy. Nor did he follow up after the party to obtain more details. Incredibly, he did not even file a memo—called an "information report"—recording that such an allegation had been made. If he had, the severe damage that later occurred to U.S. national security might never have happened.[59]

8

Each word
each joke
which his scorching mouth spews,
jumps like a naked prostitute
from a burning brothel.

—VLADIMIR MAYAKOVSKY, "A Cloud
in Trousers"

BY THE END OF 1982, Souther had received an honorable discharge from the navy and joined the naval reserve in Norfolk, Virginia. Norfolk is an idyllic port city—a quiet, clean southern town overshadowed by towering ships that come to use its deep harbor. Tall, tanned, leggy blondes parade down flower-lined avenues, and on Saturday nights sailors find their way to Waterside Festival Marketplace along the harbor to drink beer, eat barbecue and oysters, and ogle the slow-talking, miniskirted girls.

At first, Souther performed reserve duty one weekend a month at the public affairs office of the naval air station in Norfolk, Virginia. He also enrolled at Old Dominion University, majoring in Russian. Old Dominion is a state university on a 146-acre campus dotted with flowering trees and pink-brick buildings with thin rectangular windows. Originally the Norfolk division of the College of William and Mary, it was founded in

1930.[60] Souther would later confide that the Soviets had told him to take Russian to further his chances of becoming an officer and entering higher-level intelligence work.

Souther moved in with three nineteen-year-old girls who were also students at Old Dominion. They had placed an ad for a roommate and were surprised when a male responded. The house was a four-bedroom white structure at 4814 Killam Street. They called it the Little White House. Souther had a bedroom in the back. At the time, he was dating Kelli Templeton, the navy photographer from the Patuxent River naval air station. On weekends he would visit her in Maryland, or she would come to visit him in Norfolk.

To Cindy, a fresh-faced nineteen-year-old who was one of Souther's new roommates, Glenn and Kelli looked like the perfect couple.* They were the same height, looked happy together, and had the same interests. Besides photography, both liked the opera. Kelli had also interested Souther in target practice. But when Cindy told Souther they seemed to be a perfect couple, he said, "No, we're not."

"Why not?" she asked.

"You don't really know her," he said.

Then Cindy began noticing that increasingly Templeton was visiting Souther, rather than the other way around.

One night, Souther slept with Darcie A. Long, a sandy-haired, short young woman with blue eyes who was Cindy's best friend.

"When I first met him, I thought he was kind of funny and interesting. He was intelligent. He was more sophisticated than a lot of people I knew—on the surface," Long said. "I was

---

*When interviewed, Cindy agreed to having her name used in the book. However, she later requested deletion of her last name. While not obligated to accede to her request, the author did so out of appreciation for the extensive help she provided. Photographs of her appear in the book.

attracted to him, and I slept with him one time," she said.[61] "He was not much. He was an older guy. He handled it okay. It seemed like he could have gotten attached [to me], but I didn't want anything like that."

She recalled that one time Souther extended his arm to shake her hand through his open fly.

"That was an example of the geeky things he would do," Long said. "You can't help but laugh. But it's a stupid thing to do."

The day after they went to bed, Souther brought Long some flowers and a book of poetry.

Souther confided to Cindy that he was crazy about Long. He said he never really liked Templeton.

"She forced herself on me," he said. "I like her and think the world of her, but it's not deep love and someone I would marry," he said of the navy photographer.

The roommates got into a routine of studying from 7:00 P.M. to 11:00 P.M. Then as a reward, they would go for a drink at Courtney's, a local bar that had the best nachos around. After some weeks of this, the others in the house would go to sleep instead of going out. Souther and Cindy would wind up going to the bar alone.

One night on the way home from the bar, Souther began kissing Cindy in his car. She resisted, pointing out that he was still dating Kelli.

"Glenn, how can you do this?" she said. "I don't want to have anything to do with this."

But a few nights later they both became drunk, and they wound up sleeping together. While she had had sex before, she considered Souther her first serious boyfriend.[62]

Cindy was a blue-eyed, nubile blonde who wore miniskirts and no bra. She had a direct gaze, a firm handshake, and an even-toothed smile that lasted. She was open like clear glass, with no refractions and no shading. Healthy and virile, she had the overall look of a natural beauty. She had high cheekbones with a healthy blush of sun and color in her cheeks. Her mouth was parted like a heart, wide and voluptuous. She had an alert, bright look in her eyes, quick and sharp looking. Her hair was fine and blond, and her bangs fell just below her eyebrows. Her eyes were big, blue, and wide, with a look of curiosity and wonderment about them, as if she were a little girl on her first day of kindergarten. She was athletic and warm-looking, but at the same time sexy and mysterious. She looked witty and friendly and approachable, but she also looked tough, as though she wouldn't stand for anyone rubbing her the wrong way. Indeed, among her many other attributes, Cindy had a black belt in karate.

The daughter of a retired master gunnery sergeant in the marines, Cindy was born at Camp Lejeune and had had a strict upbringing. She was taught to say "Yes, sir" or "No, sir" when her father asked her questions. Like most marines, he was fiercely patriotic. When Cindy later wanted to buy a Japanese car, he told her, "If you have a foreign car, don't drive to my house."

When her sister started dating, her father cross-examined each young man she brought home.

"How come your hair is so long?" he would ask.

When he started the same routine on her, Cindy stopped dating because she was so embarrassed.[63]

One time, her father pinched a date's cheek.

"Got your shit together?" he asked him.

Another time, he was waiting on the front porch with a shotgun across his lap when Cindy and a date came home.

"Better behave yourself. Better not touch my girls!" he said.

Cindy's mother, a high school biology teacher, became worried because she was not going out. She scolded her father for bothering Cindy's dates. When she was seventeen, Cindy began dating again.

Beginning in the eighth grade in Dumfries, Virginia, Cindy had studied an Okinawa style of karate. In high school, she earned a black belt, second degree. She was so good that she took on marines who were also learning karate.

Because her instructor was also a private investigator, she became a bodyguard, protecting wealthy businessmen and people involved in marital disputes. As a private investigator, she carried a gun and was trained in its use. In addition, she used sparring gloves for full-contact karate and a sai, a vicious-looking steel hook for grabbing and striking people. Because of her proficiency, her instructor wanted her to run a new branch of his school. Along with her instructor and several other students, she appeared on the "Today" show in 1982.

"Bodyguards who don't stand out in a crowd, or maybe they do because they are beautiful," Jane Pauley said as she introduced Cindy and several other female karate experts on the show.

During the segment, Cindy's instructor broke seven concrete blocks with his head. He then broke a two-inch-by-two-inch board across Cindy's ribs. Cindy did her part. She broke five concrete bricks with the heel of her foot.

Souther was proud of her karate training. "You know she's a black belt in karate," he would tell friends.

To Cindy, Souther was the romantic a woman dreams of. Souther would take her to fancy restaurants, pull out the chair for her, and order exceptional Italian wines. He often sent her roses. For five days in a row, he would send a card saying, "I just wanted to say I love you." She would open her notebook in class to find "I love you very, very much" inscribed on several pages.

Cindy called Souther "Noodles." When he sent her cards, he signed them "Noodles."

"Sexually, he was crazy as he was in everything else he did," Cindy said. "He wanted to do it anywhere. That was a real turn-on for him. The more inappropriate the place, the more excited he would get. At first he wanted it three times a day, even during lunch. We'd go parking in his car and he would do it there, just to be different."

One day, Souther said, "Let's do it in every room in the house."

They had sex in the kitchen, in the pantry, on the stairs, and in their roommates' rooms. One time one of their roommates caught them having sex in her room.

"He wasn't happy if it wasn't risky," Cindy said. "To some extent he was a James Bond figure."

One evening, Cindy told Souther that her sister had measured her boyfriend's penis.

"Let's measure mine," he said.

It came to seven inches.

It was clear that sex formed a major part of Souther's life. He would act out different fantasies, like wearing a girl's bra, and ask Cindy to take pictures of him. But Cindy thought he wasn't exceptional in bed.

"He was just basic. Get it up, have sex, come, and that's that," she said.[64]

Meanwhile, Souther continued to see Templeton, along with other girls. Just after he became involved with Cindy, Souther's brother, Tim, came to visit. For a week the two went drinking in bars. Tim Souther was in awe of his brother's way with girls. The visit did nothing to disabuse him of that feeling. One afternoon, the two were at a gas station and saw a pretty girl with white pants pumping gas. Souther pulled up and said, "I can see your underpants."

Tim Souther was open-mouthed. Instead of taking it as an insult, the girl laughed. Anyone else would have gotten a slap, he thought to himself.

One evening, they were drinking at a quiet bar when Souther noticed two girls who turned out to be models. He went over to them and started talking to them. They ignored him. As Souther persisted, a bouncer came over to throw him out. The young women told him to get rid of Souther. Tim Souther turned the other way. When he looked again, the girls were splitting their Chinese food with Souther. One ended up taking him home.[65]

During the week, Souther spent $650 on drinks and dinners. Souther loaned his brother $150 and gave him an Italian watch worth $400. The figures stuck in Tim's mind. He wondered how his brother could afford such a life-style.

With Cindy, Souther felt he could reveal his impish side. Di Palma had frowned on his antics, calling them immature. But Cindy seemed to find them humorous, if not embarrassing.

As a prank, Souther would moon people in the street or get down on the floor and nip at the heels of waitresses.

"If we'd go out drinking, when we were just friends, he'd jump up and hug the waitresses or talk dirty to them. He was always flamboyant and would stand out. I'd get real embarrassed," Cindy said.

Cindy noticed, too, that Souther was drinking more heavily. Usually he drank Italian red wine, but sometimes he had mixed drinks, beer, or vodka that he kept in the freezer. It was during these drinking bouts that Souther began dropping hints that he was doing something illegal. The first time, they were sitting in Souther's room, which he had decorated with a Greek rug and black-and-white photos of mausoleums.

"I don't know if I want to go on with this," he blurted out. "I'd like to have a normal life with you."[66]

"What are you talking about?" she asked.

"I just don't know if I can get out of what I'm in. I'm in it too deep," he said.

Souther had been talking about going to Italy, and the first thing that crossed her mind was organized crime.

"Is it the Mafia?" Cindy asked him.

"No, no, no," he said. "I don't subscribe to anything they do. I don't believe in prostitution. I don't believe in drugs. You know I never touch drugs."

Then he changed the subject.

A few nights later, as he downed wine in Cindy's bright yellow bedroom, Souther began to repeat the same strange litany.

"I just can't go on with this. They want me to continue but I want to quit."[67]

"Who are *they*?" Cindy asked.

"I can't tell you who *they* are," he said.

"What are *they* doing?" Cindy asked.

"I can't tell you," he said.

"How did you get involved with them? What do they have to do with you?" she persisted.

He wouldn't say.

"Well, just quit."

"I'm too far into it," he said, breaking down. "I don't think I can."

"Well, what would they do, kill you? Would they pursue you?"

"I don't know what would happen," Souther said.

The same dialogue would repeat itself every few weeks. Each time, Souther would refer to "them" but refuse to say who "they" are.

"Don't ever make me tell you," he pleaded one night as they sat in his room. "My wife used to nag me to tell her, Kelli used to nag me. I'm not going to put up with it. Don't nag me," he said.

He was shaking.

Soon, Souther began talking about Stalin and Lenin, extolling them as great leaders. Cindy had grown up on a farm with a goat, chickens, and four dogs. She had no idea who the Soviet leaders were. When Souther would talk about Lenin, she would mix the man's name up with the city of Leningrad, asking, "Who was Leningrad?" Because she had no experience with spies or spying, the last thing to cross her mind was that he was a traitor to his country.

Meanwhile, Cindy was increasingly bothered by Souther's drinking. She was a psychology major, and she felt he was paranoid and on the verge of being an alcoholic. When he drank, he would talk about how much he hated his father.[68]

"My father is so money-oriented," he would say. "He wasn't there when I needed him. I can't stand him and what he represents."

As an executive at a bakery, Souther said, his father was "uppity and doesn't care about the little people."

From the way Souther described it, he had had a disturbing childhood. He said he was teased and hung out with a group nobody liked. In particular, Souther seemed to identify with a big, fat friend that everybody tormented.

"I hated them for that," he said.

The friend died when they were in junior high school, he said. Apparently, he was the cousin of Dave Glueckert, his childhood friend.

"I cried about it," Souther said.

In fact, Souther had always been popular in school. Somehow, his perception of himself had become warped, and he thought of himself as an outcast and a failure. The truth was that he was a leader and quite successful in his own world, someone whom others looked up to.

Cindy felt his pranks and bizarre behavior were a way of compensating for low self-esteem. "He wanted to be noticed," she said. "He was not satisfied with himself."

One afternoon Souther confided to Cindy that since high school he had been a chronic masturbator, to the point that he got sores on his penis and experienced pain because of the constant friction.

"Do you know you're the first person I've been with that I didn't masturbate around while I was dating?" Souther said. "I haven't done it since I knew you," he said.

"Well, maybe I'm doing something right," she thought. Later she wrote a paper in psychology about obsessive-compulsive personality disorders. She realized that Souther had a serious emotional problem.

"Obsessive personality neurosis is a personality disorder which is characterized by obsessions (unwanted thoughts, images, fears, or impulses) and compulsions (unwanted repetitive acts or conflicts, behavior patterns)," she wrote.

It seemed to her that Souther was paranoid as well. Wherever they drove, Souther would look in his rearview mirror, as if he were afraid someone was following them.

"Look at that waitress," he would say in a restaurant. "Isn't there something funny about her?" Or he would ask Cindy if she had noticed that a group had been sitting near them a long time.

"They're just drinking," she would say.

"But we moved, and then they moved," he would respond.

If a policeman pulled up behind them, he would begin turning corners to see if the officer was still following.

Between that and his drinking, Cindy was getting fed up.

He was twenty-six and she was nineteen, yet it seemed their ages were reversed. One night as they lay in bed, Cindy told him that she would have nothing more to do with him if he did not stop drinking. The threat seemed to work. He said he would quit, and his drinking diminished after that.

In May 1983, Souther and Cindy were walking together to the downtown Norfolk post office, where Souther kept a post office box. He explained that he did not want it near their house because he was afraid someone would spot him going there.

"If I wanted to go to Italy, would you want to go with me?" he asked her.

Cindy had never been outside the United States, and the idea took her aback. Souther was so unpredictable, she thought.

"Are you serious?" she asked him.

"Yeah," he said.

"I don't know. I don't know if I can afford it," she said.

Souther dropped the subject, but a few days later he brought it up again. He said he would pay for her ticket.

"I have to do things for them," he explained.

"Okay," she said.

He told her that bringing her with him would diminish suspicions. "They" had offered to provide a female companion for him, someone who worked for them and could be trusted. But he said he told them he did not want one.

"They asked me that before they checked you out," he said.

"Checked me out? What the hell is that?" she asked.

"Don't worry about it," he said.

Souther cautioned her not to tell anyone they were going to Italy. If anyone saw them traveling, she was to say they were going to visit his son.

At the time, Souther was making $144 a month from his reserve salary. He was receiving a government stipend for his educational costs. He had no other means for paying for a trip to Italy for one, let alone two.

When Cindy asked him where he got the money, Souther said, "They told me if I ever need money, I can just contact them."

Early on in their relationship, he told her "they" had left $7,000 for him in a park in Washington, but he wasn't able to find it. He called it a "drop."[69]

"I want to go back and try and look again," he said.

"How long ago was this?" she asked.

"It was before I moved down here when I was still in Maryland," he said.

"And you think $7,000 is still going to be sitting there in the park waiting for you?"

"Yes, because they hollowed out a log and put it inside, and it's in a plastic bag," he said. "They told me exactly where it was. The day I went there I couldn't find it, and I didn't stay long because there was a lot of activity going on in the park, so I left."

Souther asked Cindy to go back with him to look for it. At the last minute, he dropped her at her parents' house between Washington and Norfolk before he went to look for the money. He said it was too dangerous for her to be with him. He later reported that he hadn't found the money. But he gave her a cover story to explain why he lived better than most students.

"If anyone asks, my grandfather left me money," he said.

Before the trip to Italy, they drove to Raleigh, North Carolina, to get a copy of Cindy's birth certificate. Because it would have taken too long to apply by mail, Souther drove to Washington to apply for her passport.

"Just tell your parents we're going to Chicago," he instructed.

One night before they left, Cindy became angry that he had not told her who he was working for.

"You've got to tell me," she said.

"No," he said. "Don't ever ask me again."

Cindy decided she wouldn't. Souther had been pressing her to get married, and she had said they should wait until they had graduated. At the same time she did not want to lose him. If he had left his wife and left Kelli because they nagged him, she would not do the same thing, she decided.

9

People sniff
the smell of burnt flesh!
A brigade of men drive up.
A glittering brigade.
In bright helmets.
But no jackboots here!
Tell the firemen
to climb lovingly when a heart's on
fire.

—VLADIMIR MAYAKOVSKY, "A Cloud
in Trousers"

IN LATE MAY, Souther and Cindy flew to Rome via New York. In the plane, they fooled around under a blanket, and Souther wanted to meet Cindy in the lavatory to have sex. She refused.

At the same time, Souther was so nervous that Cindy could barely enjoy the trip. She did not know what he was afraid of, but it was contagious. He clutched his tan camera bag as if it contained an H-bomb. When they got off the plane to go through customs in Rome, he said, "Act like there's nothing wrong. If anybody stops you, show them what they want. Don't act like anything is wrong."

Cindy didn't know anything was wrong until Souther told her. After these instructions, it was impossible for Cindy to act normally. Their luggage was searched, and Souther looked as if he were about to be arrested.

"I'm not sure I want to go through with this," she whispered to him after they had cleared customs.

"Go here if I don't come back," he said, pointing to the American embassy on a map of Rome.

"Glenn, what's going to happen?" she asked.

"Don't worry," he said.

He told her he was going to the men's room. He took so long she wondered if he would ever reappear.

"Once we get out of Rome, I'll be okay," he said.

The next morning, they were in their hotel room when Souther told Cindy, "I have something I have to do. I have to meet with these people."

He told her she could walk around the city. But Cindy decided she was not leaving her room. She wondered what would happen if he did not come back. She did not have a return ticket.

Souther had told her not to drink the water, so she walked to the front desk to ask where she could get some.

"Water," she said.

They didn't understand.

She went back to her room and decided not to go out again. She sat on the bed and cried.

After six hours, Souther returned. He opened his camera bag. Inside were big wads of crisp U.S. bills.

Giving half to Cindy, Souther said, "See how much you have there."

They both counted it. Altogether it came to $10,000.[70]

"Stick some in your coat pocket," he said. He put the rest in his bag and in his inner pockets.

No big deal for the Mafia, Cindy thought. In a way, it was exciting going with someone who had such exotic connections.[71]

"Aren't you going to eat?" she asked him.

"No, I had a big dinner with them. It was great," he said.

They stayed in Rome three days, and Souther went to meet with his people once more. For the remainder of the ten-day trip, they toured Florence, Orvieto, Assisi, and Terracina in a rental car. Despite his claim that he missed his son, they never saw him.

Now that they were out of Rome, Souther seemed much more relaxed. Still, Souther would not let Cindy take a photo of him in Italy. Instead, he took pictures of the sights. He spread a map of Italy on the sidewalk and photographed their shadows outlined on it.

As they passed some shops, Souther said, "Buy whatever you want." She chose a skirt and matching top, along with a pair of leather shoes and a purse.

After they returned to Norfolk, Cindy told her friend Darcie Long that she had been to Italy, but she said very little about the trip. Nor did she show her any pictures.

"When I tried to ask her [Cindy] about it, she said, 'I was really scared. It was weird because I didn't speak the language, and when Glenn left, I was afraid to go out by myself.' I thought that was a little bit strange, but I just believed her," Long said.

Meanwhile, Templeton had been trying frantically to call Souther in Norfolk while he was in Italy with Cindy. As far as she knew, they were still going together. Carolyn Weiser, another roommate at the Little White House, would take Templeton's calls. Weiser was a plump blonde with short, curly hair. She and her boyfriend, Robert Graham, often double-dated with Souther and Templeton, having brunch at the Pot Pourri, Souther's favorite restaurant. Or they would visit the Hermitage Foundation Museum, an English Tudor mansion that displays rare western and Oriental art treasures. On Sunday nights, they would cook dinner at home, often with Cindy. Graham was in the navy also, and he asked Cindy to teach him some karate moves. She agreed and told him she would begin by hitting him in the chest lightly.

"That's light?" he had said when she knocked the wind out of him.

Weiser was bemused by Souther's cooking style. He insisted on the health benefits of steaming meat, and he would often preside over the preparations.

"With frozen meat, you have to thaw it out," Souther explained. "You can steam it and not thaw it out beforehand. Put a little water in the bottom. Put all the vegetables in, and don't lift the top. It takes twenty minutes."

He would get mad if anyone lifted the lid to peek.

Through these encounters, Weiser became friends with Templeton. Weiser hated having to lie to her about Souther's relationship with Cindy. She never understood what someone as refined and mature as Templeton saw in Souther anyway.

Early on, an incident occurred that convinced her that Souther had a few screws loose. A tape deck and some tapes had been stolen from Souther's red Renault. Souther was frantic about the theft, trying to find out if anything else had been taken from the car. As a prank, Weiser's boyfriend, Graham, thought it would be funny to move Souther's car and pretend it had also been stolen. When Souther went to the car with Templeton and discovered it was gone, he came back to the apartment in a frenzy.

"Glenn, lost your car lately?" Graham asked him.

Weiser realized he was going off the deep end and whispered to Cindy that they should tell him where his car was. Before they could say anything, Souther grabbed a hunting knife and held it to Graham's face.[72] Everyone began yelling at him.

Inexplicably, Souther then pushed Templeton up against a

68

wall, swore at her, and told her to go back to Maryland. She went in his bedroom with him, and he came out crying.

"Pack up and leave," Weiser told Souther.

But Souther turned on his charm and apologized profusely. Later, Cindy learned that his car had something to do with his spying.

Another time, Cindy introduced a date to Souther. The young man noticed a photograph Souther had taken of Templeton.

"It's a beautiful picture," the date said.

Souther turned around angrily.

"It? It? That's a she," Souther said.

"Sorry," the date said. "I just thought it was a nice picture."

One night Souther heard a noise outside the house. He pulled out a handgun and shouted, "I'm going to shoot!"

"Glenn, we're in a big city. Anyone could be walking by," Cindy said.

While he often acted in a bizarre way, Souther could also be exceptionally thoughtful. When she found out the navy was transferring her boyfriend overseas, Weiser began crying inconsolably in her closet so no one would hear. Souther was in the bathroom adjoining the closet and heard her.

"He comforted me and poured me some wine," Weiser said. "He could be intelligent, violent, immature. He was a lot of complex people."

Weiser did not know Souther and Cindy were traveling together, but by the time they got back, she had figured it out. She resented having been lied to. Before Souther and Cindy had started going with each other, everyone at the Little White House had been friends. Now everyone was secretive and suspicious. To get back at them, Weiser skipped classes when she knew they would be coming back. She sat in the living room and smiled when they both showed up together.

A few days later, Templeton called the house and asked for Souther. Since he was then in the shower with Cindy, Weiser told her he was not in.

"Whenever I call, Glenn's not there," Templeton said. "I have a feeling something's going on. Is he seeing someone?

"I really don't want to get involved in this," Weiser said.

"Carolyn, you're my friend," Templeton said. "Is he seeing somebody?"

"Yes."

"Is it Cindy?"

"Yes."[73]

"I'm on my way down," Templeton said.

When she got to the house, Weiser told Templeton she might want to take a look at a photo album in Cindy's room. Despite Souther's proscription against taking pictures of themselves in Italy, the album contained one photo of Souther and Cindy together. At a restaurant outside of Rome, a professional photographer had snapped a picture of them with a Polaroid camera. Souther had flipped out, waving him away frantically. But the man took it anyway and gave it to Souther without charging him.

Templeton was furious when she saw it. She gave Weiser twenty dollars to leave the house and get her hair done at a nearby beauty parlor.

"I won't let them know you told me," she whispered.

When she got back, Templeton was crying.

"I know a lot about you. I can get you," Weiser heard her saying to Souther.[74]

Souther tried to comfort her, but Templeton soon stormed out of the house.

By now, the once friendly roommates had installed big locks on their doors, and they whispered when they were on the phone. Cindy considered Weiser to be a busybody.

70

In August, Souther moved into his own apartment in Norfolk's Ghent section, known for its artists and homosexuals.
Cindy moved in with him. She stored most of her belongings
at a friend's house, returning every few days to get fresh
clothes.[75] When she was seven, her mother had explained the
facts of life to her with the help of a chart. But Cindy was afraid
of what her father would say if he knew she was living with a
man.

10

Mama!
I cannot sing.
In the heart's chapel the choir loft
catches fire!

—VLADIMIR MAYAKOVSKY, "A Cloud
    in Trousers"

BESIDES his spying activities and his romantic attachments, Souther led still another life—that of an overgrown college student. By now he was attending Old Dominion University full-time while performing his naval reserve duty on weekends. The nucleus of that other life was the Russian Club, a group of fifteen Old Dominion students majoring, like Souther, in Russian.

Danine D. Klein, a comely fellow Russian student who was the club's treasurer, became particularly close to him. Klein was an intellectual and a mensch, a person of integrity and honor whom you would want on your side when going into any battle. She was natural-looking, with a warm, sunny look to her and smooth, shapely legs. Her eyes were light brown to hazel and happy-looking, her cheeks rosy with health. She had brown hair and bangs. She was fun to be around, talkative, friendly, and open. If she were your friend, she would do anything for you and think nothing of it.

Souther ran into her in a first-floor lounge at Old Dominion's College of Arts and Letters in January 1983. Klein's purse was resting on a nearby table, and Souther reached into it and pulled out a box of tampons.

Waving the box in the air to attract the attention of other students, he said, "What's this for, Danine?"

Klein could not believe it. Here was a twenty-six-year-old man acting like a ten-year-old boy. After that, she didn't speak to him for six months. Then in June she relented. Souther had apologized each time he saw her, and he finally sent her a sweet card begging her forgiveness.[76]

They became platonic friends.

With great relish, Souther would regale Klein with the details of his sexual conquests and his opinions of his Russian teachers and the small coterie of students that formed their social group. He was candid with her about his own shortcomings, admitting that he had hemorrhoids and flat feet. He told her he felt he had a weak chin, which he tried to cover with a beard.

Playing a Wendy to his Peter Pan, Klein took perverse pleasure in seeing how effectively Souther pricked the shells that people built around themselves. She admired the fact that he would say what he thought to whomever he wanted; he was not afraid to be himself. She took delight in his tendency to flout conventions.

Eventually, Souther's increasingly bizarre behavior would contribute to the denial of his officer's commission. But for now it provided a release from the nerve-racking pressures of his spy activities.

John A. Fahey, Souther's adviser and one of his two Russian

teachers, recalled that Souther would use obscene language and sexual innuendos in class. "He was intelligent, keen, and quick," Fahey said. "He caught on quickly and had a good mind. But he was sort of wild. He would tell off-color jokes and engage in pranks I couldn't accept. I would come ten minutes before the class started. He would be horsing around."

A retired naval commander, Fahey had been a pilot and later head of the navy's language school. Souther wanted to be a naval officer, and one day Fahey took him aside.

"How are you going to be a naval officer if you use obscene language like that?" Fahey asked him.

"Everyone in the navy talks like that," Souther said.

"No, I don't think so," Fahey said.

"The navy's changed since you were in it," Souther said.

"If you're an officer, the commanding officer will note you fast, and you won't advance one rank with the sort of behavior you have," Fahey said.

Souther listened, and after that Fahey had no more problems with him.[77]

Souther's other professor, Dr. Leonid I. Mihalap, was a Russian émigré. Like Fahey, Mihalap was impressed by Souther and saw something of himself in him.

"Basically he behaved the same way I would have behaved when you have to maintain maturity in chronological age when your classmates are younger," he said.[78]

Souther led both professors to believe he was a superpatriot. "He loved the U.S. at least as much as I do. He was ready to give his life for his country, as I would now without hesitation," Mihalap said. "There was never any doubt in my mind."

Klein had gone to a Quaker high school and was taught to see the military as evil. She and Souther often argued about U.S. policy. Souther defended the U.S. invasion of Grenada and denounced the Soviet invasion of Afghanistan. When Klein urged him to sign a petition protesting U.S. policy in El Salvador, Souther refused.

"You never know where lists like that will end up," he said.[79]

Souther never talked about what he did in the navy, saying it was secret. But he complained that enlisted men were abused—something Klein had heard from many others in the navy.[80]

"He would say they had to scrub the floor with a toothbrush or polish things that were already shining," Klein said. "He talked about how miserable he was and what assholes the officers were to the enlisted men. He said he wanted to change the system from within. He wanted to become an officer so he could change it—be a good one and not be an asshole."

When he had reserve duty, Souther would shave his beard and don his uniform. Once he called Klein from the naval base.

"I thought you were busy this weekend," Klein said.

"I am," he said. "I'm protecting your country from Communist invasion and protecting your lily-white bosom."[81]

Souther loved to play with the electronic garage-door opener in Klein's car. Each time she picked him up, he would grab it and aim it at her, as if it were a gun.

Each member of the Russian Club took a Russian name. Glenn became Gleb. A girl named Natalia would become Natasha. John would become Ivan.

The club members would meet once a month at their professors' homes or at the homes of their parents. In between, they gave parties and hung out at the Classroom. Across the street from the main campus, the Classroom was a pine-paneled pub with a pinball machine and a menu that included several dozen foreign beers. Usually, the members of the club spoke Russian to one another, thereby excluding the outside world.

Souther's parties always had plenty of food and drink. They were hot, sweaty affairs, with loud music and exceptionally nice food—oysters wrapped in bacon, for example. Souther would invite his neighbors to make sure they didn't complain about the noise.

Frances Higger, his apartment manager, said he was unusually considerate. "When he would have a party in his apartment, he would ask me first," she said.

Souther's apartment was an efficiency at Pelham Place, a yellow-brick, three-story garden apartment complex shaded by trees on Olney Road. He kept it immaculately clean and orderly—some thought compulsively so. There was a sofa bed with a wood frame and a bright-green-and-white pattern. The chairs were arranged just so. There was not a speck of dust anywhere, not anything out of place. On one wall was the photo he had taken of Di Palma giving birth to their son, the edges fuzzed up. On another wall was a poster commemorating Norfolk's June Harborfest, with its tall ships, fireworks, raw bars, and boat races.

Souther paid $225 a month rent. At first, he had taken a one-bedroom model at $250 a month, but claimed he could no longer afford it. However, the efficiency had the advantage of being at the front of the complex, so Souther could see anyone approaching. At the time, it was the only available apartment with a front view.[82]

Despite his claims of poverty, Klein thought Souther spent well beyond the means of a college student whose education was financed by the GI Bill. He would buy expensive red wines and tailored clothes imported from Italy, frequently pick up the tab for their meals, and take Cindy and others out to the Pot Pourri, a continental restaurant with prices that most college students could not afford. When Klein asked him about it, he said he had saved money while he was in the navy.

Christopher L. Philips, another friend from the Russian Club, recalled that Souther usually picked up the tab when they went drinking together and always seemed to have plenty of cash. When Philips was short of money, Souther loaned him $300 in crisp, new bills and made it clear he did not expect repayment any time soon. Philips gave him the money back a year later.[83]

Despite his ability to charm his teachers, many students were turned off by his blunt approach. "He would meet a girl and say, 'Hi. My name's Glenn. Would you like to go to bed with me tonight?' " Klein said. "He would say it grinning like a devil. Usually it offended women, but not for long. It might not get them into bed that night but they would be charmed by his brashness and they would become friends with him and eventually go to bed with him."

At other times, Souther would say, "I have nine and a half feet of throbbing pleasure between my legs. How would you like to experience that?"

"They were people he didn't know or hardly knew," Klein said. "Some were offended, some laughed, and some just rolled their eyes. He managed to charm enough to have a harem of women around him."

Souther's answer to everything, she said, was "You just need to get laid, or I just need to get laid, or she just needs to get fucked."

Philips first met Souther when he went to one of his parties with Andrea C. McGill, another Russian Club member. McGill looked like the cheerleader that every boy was after in high school, the flirt whom no one could get a date with. She looked like she would say no to everyone, but would secretly say yes to one. Her blond hair fell below her shoulders and was thick and soft-looking. Usually, it was in a ponytail. When she smiled her whole face lit up. She had a natural beauty with round eyes, high cheekbones, fresh skin, and a guileless smile. At other times she could look seductive, with a come-and-get-me look.

She had a curvy figure, with the toned legs of someone who exercises.

"I knocked on the door," Philips said. "Glenn opened the door, saw Andrea, and in the true wild-man style he displays, turned around, dropped his pants, bent over, and made a vulgar, disgusting homosexual remark about meeting me in this way."[84]

Souther would often joke about homosexuals, his own hemorrhoids, and the size of his sex organ. He liked to go to gay bars just to see something different. Souther's off-color sense of humor held a vague attraction for Philips.

"It shows directness and a willingness to suspend the conventions of the day and be lewd and disgusting for the sake of fun," he said. "Because he had a dynamic personality, people would find he had a redeeming side to him."

"A lot of people wondered if he was a homosexual just because of his appearance—small frame, sharp, delicate features," Klein said. "He didn't act effeminate but didn't act like the average man either. He was very profeminist. A lot of his attraction to women was that he did have respect for them. He was very supportive and interested in women. He really loved women, and that was part of his success with them. He was genuinely interested and caring."

When Klein came down with the flu just before a Russian Club party, Souther visited her at her apartment the next morning and helped her out of bed, washed her face, and gave her coffee and orange juice. She loved the smell of his Italian cologne.

Once, Souther showed Klein the cache of lambskin condoms he kept in a closet.

"He always bragged about how he took the responsibility for birth control in any relationship," Klein said. "He always said he wore a condom when having sex. He said women have so many other things to worry about in that area. He didn't even ask. He assumed it was his responsibility. It impressed the girls a lot. That's something women never hear from men."

Souther told Klein that Di Palma was spoiled, came from a rich family, was very demanding, and began cheating on him.

"He couldn't tolerate it," she said.[85]

But knowing Souther, she wondered if it had been the other way around.

He also told her that he never wanted to see his father again.

"As far as I'm concerned, I have no father," he said.

"You should forgive and forget," she told him. "Life goes on."

11

Into the calm of an apartment
where people quake,
a hundred-eyed blaze bursts from the
docks.
Moan
into the centuries,
if you can, a last scream: I'm on fire!

—VLADIMIR MAYAKOVSKY, "A Cloud
    in Trousers"

WHEN he moved to his new apartment in Ghent, Souther told Cindy, "I'm so glad to get away from people. I'm afraid they'll find something."

Souther told her he often stashed money in a couch cushion. "Now nobody can look for anything and find anything," he said.

Several times, he told her he loved her and wanted to settle down.

"I want to get out. I don't know if I can keep doing this. All I want to do is have a normal life and get married," he said.

But those moments of indecision were fleeting, and Souther would always resume his furtive existence. Even his choice of apartments seemed to be dictated by security considerations. Cindy had wanted an open, sunny apartment with lots of windows. Souther chose one that had one window.

When he bought a Commodore computer, Souther told

Cindy, "If anybody asks you, my dad sent me the money." He used the computer for writing papers but also had a modem. At other times, he said Cindy should say his grandfather had died and left some money for Souther in a trust fund.[86]

"He would just go out and buy whatever he wanted, whatever, whenever he wanted," she said. "He would pay in cash."

Souther always wanted to go out to eat. He wanted to pay, but she wanted to go Dutch. She didn't want to become totally dependent on him, but he always insisted on ordering the best wines, and she never caught up with his spending.

When Souther received payment for his reserve duty, he made sure to run the money through his checking account to create a record of receiving legitimate funds. At the time, he was receiving $144 a month for his reserve duty and $460 a month from the GI Bill. After paying his tuition of $419 a month, he had $185 left. From that he had to pay rent of $225 a month and eventually child support of $120 a month, leaving him $160 a month short. Thus he had no money left for buying food, imported wine, imported Italian clothing, or Russian books. Nor was there money for telephone service, the upkeep of his car, or entertainment, including the Three Stooges movies he loved.[87]

No money, that is, except from the KGB. Souther admitted to Di Palma that he was working for the Soviets—whom he referred to as "them"—and that they gave him money after the birth of their son. Cindy saw him receive money that he said he got from "them."

One afternoon as they sat around his coffee table, Souther showed Cindy some sheets of thin paper the size of baseball cards.

"Do you want to see something real neat?" he said.

He held out the papers and lit a match. As the flame moved toward the paper, it ignited in a puff of smoke.

"Wait a minute," Souther said. "This is wrong. This isn't supposed to leave any ashes."

Souther decided he must have burned too many sheets at the same time.

"You're only supposed to burn one at a time," he said. Then he said, "That's a big relief. I'm no longer a keeper of the numbers."

"What?" Cindy said. "What are you talking about?"

"For a long time, I was in charge of these numbers. Now somebody else is, so I don't have to watch them anymore. Thank God. It's a big relief off my shoulders."[88]

Cindy realized that Souther was talking about some kind of code. But like so much of what he said, it never made a big impression on her.

"This is why I was so sensitive when my car was broken into," he told her then. "I kept the numbers in my car in a place where no one would find them."

Just then the phone rang. Souther had an answering machine, and he told Cindy to let the caller leave a message. Souther almost always screened his calls. When the caller hung up without leaving a message, he said, "I wonder if someone is trying to contact me."

"It's somebody who doesn't want to leave a message," Cindy said.

"No," he said. "It's happening too much. Someone is trying to contact me."

Cindy told him he was being paranoid, but Souther went through the same routine whenever the phone rang. When he got messages, he would play them over and over.

A few days later, Cindy and Souther picked up the mail at the post office, and Cindy noticed a postcard for Souther from California.

"Wish you were here," it said on the back.

When Cindy asked about it, Souther was evasive.

"It's just nothing," he said.

"Just nothing?" she asked.

"Just someone trying to contact me."

"It doesn't say anything. How do you know what they want?"

"I know what they want."

"Is it them?"

"Yeah."

"Who are these people?" she said.

Souther grabbed the card from her hands. She never saw it again.[89]

One weekend, she noticed him writing a letter with a special pen that used invisible ink. After he had finished writing, she noticed that the paper looked blank. Then she saw him write over what he had written with normal ink.

"How do they know to look under the writing?" she asked.

"Oh, they know," he said.

The news came on, and Souther began railing about the U.S. government.

"That's not true," he said of the latest government pronouncement on defense. "Americans are so ignorant. They have no idea what goes on around them. They can't speak a foreign language."

"That's true, but I don't hate them for it," Cindy thought to herself. Then Souther went on about the level of education and commitment in the United States.

"A lot of people don't vote. I can't believe they don't vote," he said.[90]

"You wouldn't believe what the U.S. does," he went on. "I can't tell you the things that I do and see in my job, but you wouldn't believe it. They're so corrupt. They have everybody fooled."

Once when they were out jogging, Souther remarked that

no one would believe how much the United States controls Italy—even what Italians import and export.

"We're not a democracy," he said. "We control the whole world."

He said he loved Italy because to him it was so divided and unaggressive.

"You have all these little political groups," he said. "They are the underdog."[91]

Souther constantly talked about nuclear testing and aerial photos he had seen. He said they showed that the United States secretly tests nuclear weapons close to major cities.

"If you knew about it, it would make you sick," he said.

"The U.S. is so afraid of Russia, but the U.S. has nothing to worry about, because Russia is so far behind us," he said. "They have little water access. They're very backward. They couldn't mobilize an army because they have so many different languages. The land is icy and barren and hard to get across."

It was clear to Cindy that Souther detested the United States and admired Communism. He now had an extensive library of books about Communism. He told her he had stayed on a kibbutz in Israel while taking pictures for a navy paper. It seemed to him that the communal life-style was ideal. Next to that, he said, "Communism is the perfect form of government. People help people; you don't have poverty."

Then he went on about the navy.

"The navy makes me sick," he told her. "You have to kiss the admirals' asses."

Souther said that admirals asked him to take personal pictures of weddings.

"I can't believe they do that," he said. "I'm supposed to take photos for the navy, not of their daughters' weddings."

"It's not how good you are, it's how good a brown-noser you are," he said.

"If you don't brown-nose, how come you get promotions?" Cindy asked him.

"They like me being me. I'm honest and frank with them, and they like that," he said. "But if there's a war, I'd go to another country and never fight."

"You don't have much of a choice," she said.

"No. I have a choice. These people guaranteed me they would get me out."

At the same time, Souther would talk about his ambition of becoming an officer in the navy. If Cindy had reflected on his feelings about Communism and the U.S. government, she would have realized that he did not make sense.

Cindy decided Souther was not involved in the Mafia but was probably starting some left-wing or Communist political movement. Perhaps they wanted him to become the leader of the movement, she mused. At times, he talked about being a U.S. senator, so she thought he might want to change things from the inside. But she didn't give it much thought. As far as Cindy was concerned, the less Souther talked about his political beliefs, the better. Because she was so naïve politically, she never connected his attitudes with spying.

Indeed, even though she considered her father to be a "hard-core" marine and a superpatriot, Cindy occasionally mentioned to him that Souther had described Communism as having many good points.

"What do you think you're talking about?" he would shout, as if he were a drill instructor at boot camp. "What do you think you're saying?"[92]

"He thinks some aspects of Communism are good. What's so bad about that? Communism is just a belief. It's just a type of government," she would say.

In retrospect, she realized her father was right: she did not know what she was talking about.

In the fall of 1983, Souther told Cindy that investigators from the Defense Department would be calling her and asking for information so his security clearance could be upgraded to top secret. This was a preliminary step to his entering intelligence work. In addition, Souther was to be given access to sensitive compartmented information (SCI), which includes intelligence from spy satellites and communications and signals intercepts. For this level of clearance, the Defense Investigative Service does what is known as a special background investigation, which is even more extensive than the investigation required for a top-secret clearance.

The investigation includes a check with all federal agencies, including the FBI, CIA, and NSA, to see if their files contain any derogatory information on the individual. In addition, the DIS checks the Defense Central Index of Investigations, a computerized record of all investigations conducted by agencies of the Defense Department. The DIS also checks with private credit bureaus. Beyond that, the investigation entails interviews with the subject, former employers, and friends going back to the subject's eighteenth birthday. Investigators also verify the subject's birth and education and look into where he or she lived, foreign travel, foreign connections, and affiliations with organizations. They even check out the subject's spouse or living companion. In the case of navy personnel, the clearance for SCI access can only be issued with the approval of the commander of the Naval Intelligence Command or the Naval Security Group Command.[93]

Cindy could tell Souther was nervous about it. For days, he coached her on how to respond.

"Don't volunteer anything," he said. "Just answer their questions. Don't go into detail."

Cindy had pictured being questioned for several hours. Instead, it seemed more like a five-minute job interview for a job at K mart.

"Is this where he goes to school? Is this where he lives?" the investigator asked over the phone.

Cindy managed to answer without mentioning Souther's covert activities or his feelings of disdain for America. She knew Souther admired Communism, but she could truthfully say he was not a member of the Communist Party. Nor did she realize at the time that the money she had seen came from the Soviets. She answered "no" to all the sensitive questions and felt that everything she had said was true. So far as she knew, he had never been associated with the Communist Party.

In October 1983, Souther took Cindy to Chicago, where he obtained a divorce from Di Palma. Under the agreement, he paid $120 a month in child support. As a student, his lawyer had told Di Palma, that was all he could afford.

Occasionally, he talked about his son and how much he wanted to see him. Then he broke down and cried. But he never tried to see him, never even wrote him a letter. Cindy wondered if his feelings were sincere or if he was putting on an act to get attention. What counts is actions, not words, she thought. She marveled at how manipulative he could be. As if to prove the point, he told her that he had gotten a job at a local store while he was drunk, just to see if he could do it. Then he quit.

Despite his ability to charm people, Cindy felt that the real Glenn Souther lived inside a shell. Outside, he was fun-loving and always cracking jokes. Inside, he was crying.

12

In silence the street pushed torment.
A shout stood erect in the gullet.
Wedged in the throat,
bulging taxis and bony cabs bristled.
Pedestrians have trodden my chest
flatter than consumption.

—VLADIMIR MAYAKOVSKY, "A Cloud
    in Trousers"

IN JANUARY 1984, Souther took Cindy to Italy again. This time he said he was not sure if "they" knew he was coming.

"I've tried to contact them and haven't gotten a response," he said.[94]

The first night, they had dinner in Rome. Souther said he would spray-paint a signal on a bridge to let them know that they should contact him. After dinner, they walked together through the dark streets, and Cindy shivered. Souther seemed just as nervous as he had been on their first trip, and she remembered what he had said about going to the embassy if something happened to him.

As they walked over a stone overpass, Souther told her to wait under a streetlight. Carrying a can of red spray paint in a bag, he walked to the level below and painted a mark on a bridge pier.[95] Then they walked several blocks to a construction site, where Souther tossed the paint can. When they got back to the hotel, Cindy was a nervous wreck.

The next day, Souther said he had to do something for "them." He returned that afternoon, looking exhausted. When Cindy asked what had happened, he said, "I had to go from subway to subway and walk blocks out of my way to make sure I wasn't being followed.

"They're really good," he continued. "I was concerned about visiting twice a year and spending time on studying and going to summer school. They said not to worry about it. Things are getting shaky. They don't want twice-a-year trips anyway. They said just concentrate on Russian. Don't worry about doing something for them. If I need money, let them know."[96]

He met with them again the next day, bringing back another wad of money. He said it was $10,000.

"What if you get caught?" Cindy asked Souther.

"That's okay. They gave me something," he said.

She got the impression it was a poison pill.

During the trip, Souther bought Cindy a red wool coat with matching hat and mittens. They took the train to Florence and later visited Cindy's father's family near Pisa. This time, he allowed pictures to be taken of them together. She took one of him sitting next to a nun on the train.

"The reason we're coming is to visit your relatives," he coached her.

When a friend of Cindy's relatives showed up for a glass of wine, Souther became suspicious of him.

"I don't like him," he said.

"Glenn, he's my relatives' friend," she said. "He's not into anything or near anything."

Cindy's father had warned her that his relatives were good Catholics. "Now make sure you behave yourself," he had told

----

her. "If they go to church, you go to church with them." He gave her a cross to bring to them. But it turned out they were not any more religious than she was.

As a courtesy to her family, Souther and Cindy slept in separate bedrooms. But Cindy thought her relatives didn't care.

By then, Souther and Cindy were arguing a lot. In contrast to his attentiveness during the early part of their relationship, Souther now seemed indifferent.

"How come you aren't paying attention to me?" Cindy would complain.

He had said he would buy her an engagement ring in Europe, but never brought it up again. It seemed to her he was now just going through the motions with her. At the same time, he had stopped questioning whether he should continue to work for "them."

When they returned to Norfolk, Cindy noticed that Souther was spending more time with the members of the Russian Club. In particular, he seemed to be studying a lot with Danine Klein.

"Are you having an affair?" Cindy asked him one night. "Who is it? Is it with Danine?"

"No, no," he said. "I don't know what you're talking about."

Cindy wanted to believe him, so she let it go.

In February 1984, Cindy told Souther she would be out with her girlfriends that night. Since she had kept her own apartment, she did not always stay with Souther.

"If you decide to come back, I'll be here," he said in his apartment.

She decided to return, but found he wasn't there. Every few hours she would wake up, hoping to see him. By morning she was hysterical. She called hospitals and ambulance services. A friend of Souther's said he had seen him at a party and might have had a meeting with "his people" after that.

"Did he contact them?" he asked.

From this remark, Cindy concluded that the friend knew about Souther's covert activities.[97] The friend would later deny it to investigators.

Then one Friday evening in March 1984, Cindy and a friend walked into the Classroom, the pub across the street from Old Dominion. They passed under the red apple that was the club's insignia. It was happy hour. Cindy saw Souther and Klein sitting in a rear booth. He was kissing her hand and arm.[98] Cindy could not believe it. She knew that he was into kissing and hugging in public, but this seemed to her to go beyond that. A few months ago, Souther had wanted to marry her. He had been doing the pursuing. Now it seemed the other way around. Heartbroken, Cindy turned around and walked out.

Klein has maintained she never had an affair with Souther. She already had a boyfriend, did not like the way he treated his girlfriends, and found his skinny body unappealing. But Cindy was convinced they were having an affair.

As she walked to the car, Cindy's friend said she should turn around and confront Souther. Cindy marched back to the pub. As she approached their table, Souther and Klein were getting up.

"Hi," he said. "We were just leaving."

Cindy was stunned. She had been living with Souther for eleven months, and this was all he could say.

Cindy turned around and walked out. She drove to Souther's apartment and began stuffing her clothes into plastic trash bags. She had been there only a few minutes when Souther walked in. He and Klein had just driven up in separate cars, and Klein was driving off.

"Let's talk," Souther said.

He has a nerve, Cindy thought.

Cindy left and stayed that weekend with her parents. She had always thought that if he went out on her, she would not

----

return. But on Tuesday, she called him and said, "I don't know what I did wrong, but let's try again."

"Okay, let's try it," he said.

"I'm really sorry," he said to her when she came back. "I didn't mean to hurt you."

Cindy asked about Klein. He did not deny having an affair with her, and he seemed cold and unfeeling about it. "Let's just drop it," he said.

"How long has this been going on?" she asked.

"I can't say," he said.

"Have you slept with her?"

"I'm not going to tell you. I'd rather not," he said.

That Friday, Cindy went out with Darcie Long. She told Long that Souther said he would stop seeing Klein. But she was suspicious and upset. She insisted on going to his house to see if he was there. Long waited outside in the car. When Cindy opened the door, she saw Klein sitting on the sofa bed.

Cindy was livid.

"Nothing is going on," Souther said. "She just stopped by to talk to me."

According to Klein, Souther had said he wasn't sure if he would be attending a Russian Club party that night. He told Klein to drop by so she could take him. Souther had wrecked his car and now rode his bicycle everywhere.[99]

Cindy began crying. Frantically, she tried to kick him in the testicles. She did not use her karate techniques. Instead, she flailed at him.

"If you don't stop, I'm going to hit you," he warned her.

She continued to hit at him ferociously, and finally, after several warnings, he punched her in the face. Blood came streaming from her mouth.[100]

"I'm really sorry," he said. "You made me do that."

Cindy and Klein left. As Klein was pulling out of the parking lot in her Volkswagen Rabbit, Long demanded to know what she had done to provoke such a fight. Klein ignored her and drove off. Long then got out of the car, went back into the apartment, and started screaming at Souther. Then she left.

Cindy later had to have root-canal work done on her two front teeth, which had turned black from internal bleeding. Souther offered to pay for it. Cindy declined, saying it was her fault.

"I went in and attacked you," she said.

Souther would later tell Klein he was thankful Cindy had not used her karate techniques.

Beyond a brief encounter on campus, Souther and Cindy never saw each other again. With the exception of a Russian matrushka doll, the only memento she had of their relationship was a copy of *Ethan Frome,* by Edith Wharton.

"To you, from me," he had inscribed it. She never understood why Souther liked it. To her, it was a depressing tale— of unrequited love in a snowy, New England setting, and of a small deception that led to disaster.

Even though she saw him again only briefly, it would not be the end of her involvement in his case.

13

But the street, squatting down, bawled:
"Let's go and guzzle!"

—VLADIMIR MAYAKOVSKY, "A Cloud
in Trousers"

AT 7:25 P.M. on Monday, April 2, 1984, Cynthia M. Kotulak, a freshman at Old Dominion, was walking to her room in the girls' wing of Gresham Hall, a brick dormitory on Forty-ninth Street, to pick up a bus schedule. Suddenly, Deborah Biehler, a friend who was walking with her, yelled out a warning: "Cindy!"[101]

Before she knew it, Glenn Souther had jumped her and pinned her arms to the floor. Then he began biting her neck. Kotulak was in pain and could not get up.

"Stop it! Stop it!" she yelled.

Meanwhile, a friend of Souther's pinned Biehler against a wall as she tried to help Kotulak. Eventually, Souther let Kotulak go. She ran into her room, only to be pursued by Souther, who pushed his way in.

"Stop it! What are you doing?" Kotulak yelled.

Biehler had never met Souther, and Kotulak had met him

94

only once briefly, a week earlier. She knew nothing about his penchant for pranks. To her, he was a twenty-seven-year-old man who had just assaulted her. She thought he had gone haywire.[102]

Just before the incident, Souther had been drinking beer with Danine Klein and several other members of the Russian Club at the B&R Railroad, a pub across the street from the Old Dominion campus. A derelict wandered in—a big, beefy man who reminded Klein of Richard Speck, who had been convicted in 1966 of murdering eight student nurses at a Chicago college dormitory. The man started making trouble, yelling at the patrons. Then he began wisecracking with Souther, and Souther goaded him on, talking right back to him, daring him to come after him. The man threatened to kill Souther. Finally, the manager called the police, who took the derelict away.[103]

Now Souther was terrorizing Kotulak, who demanded that he leave her room. When he refused, she picked up a tennis racket and held it ready to hit him. Souther picked up a wrench lying nearby and threatened her.

"Let's rearrange a few things," he said.

Grabbing the tennis racket from Kotulak, Souther accidentally struck Biehler in the face with it.

"Get out!" Kotulak shouted again.

Finally, the two women managed to push Souther and his friend out the door. Kotulak locked the door, only to see Souther reenter Kotulak's room through a bathroom that adjoined her room. He later said he intended to apologize, but she screamed at him to leave, and he did.

Kotulak looked in the mirror. She had a bite mark on her neck. While the bite had not penetrated her skin, the red mark—which looked like a hickey—remained for two weeks.[104]

Kotulak and Biehler told the dormitory assistant, who called the Old Dominion campus police. Lieutenant Ellen M. Lucas responded to the call. When Lucas got to the dorm, she found both young women still trembling. In the dorm assistant's room on the first floor, they told her what had happened. They said they wanted to file a complaint. Lucas examined the red mark on Kotulak's neck and called the Norfolk city police. She also called Response, an independent center that helps women involved in sexual assaults.[105]

Meanwhile, Lucas found Souther and asked him if he had a lawyer.

"No," he said. "I don't need one. This is ridiculous."

The next morning, the city police picked up Souther and booked him. He spent several hours in jail before he was released on bail.

That night, Souther told Klein that he had been put in the same cell with the derelict who had threatened him at the B&R Railroad.

"Here I was in jail for the first time in my life, and the one person in the entire city of Norfolk they put me with is the man that wants to kill me," he said. But Souther said they ended up the best of friends.

The derelict told Souther, "We've been wronged by society."

"I hope you've learned your lesson," Klein said. "Pulling pranks like that can get you in trouble."

"No, no, I'll never change," Souther said. "Nothing will make me grow up."

But the next day Souther ran into Katherine Byrd, a fellow Old Dominion student who had been the victim of a similar attack by Souther the previous year. At the time, they were both attending the Last Class Bash, a traditional Old Dominion party held outside just before final exams. They were lying on blankets, and Souther began making advances on her. When she rejected him, he went after her.

"He bit me on the thigh, and it hurt," she later said.[106]

Unlike Kotulak, she fought back, kicking him hard.

When Souther later saw her, he told her he was worried he would be suspended for biting Kotulak.

A few days later, at a National Slavic Honor Society function attended by all the members of the Russian Club, Souther went up to his friends and began growling like a bear, snapping his jaws to demonstrate what a threat he was.[107]

Soon the Kotulak case became a cause célèbre on campus, with students lining up to attack or defend Souther or Kotulak. To those who knew Souther, it was inconceivable that he would hurt anyone. He was always clowning around, always on the cutting edge of the latest craze; they thought Kotulak was over-reacting and trying to ruin his life for no reason.

Cheryl D. Oberg was one who was outraged by what Kotulak had done. Oberg was known as "Purple" because she dressed in purple and even had a purple phone. She knew Souther through her roommate, E. King Butterworth, a member of the Russian Club. Oberg's room was near Kotulak's, and she had come on the scene just after Souther bit Kotulak in the hall.

The next day, she went to Kotulak's room and asked her why she was pressing charges.

"When I asked her why she was doing it, she shrugged," Oberg said. "I said, 'Did he scare you?' She said no. Being a woman, I said, 'Did you feel threatened that your body was in danger?' She said no. I said, 'Then why in God's name are you doing this? Why can't it just be dropped? He meant no harm.'"

It seemed to Oberg that someone must have been urging Kotulak to pursue the case.

"She wasn't upset," Oberg said. "It seemed she didn't know why she was doing it, but she was doing it."[108]

But Kotulak had a different version. She said she told Oberg and others that Souther had terrified her and hurt her. No one urged her to press charges, she said. What infuriated her was the campus reaction. Instead of blaming Souther, students were blaming her.

"I'd be sitting down to dinner and hear people coming by with comments: 'God, how could she do that to that guy?' Or 'Better get out of here; she may cry rape.' "[109]

"One time two of them tried to talk me out of it," she said. " 'How can you do this and ruin his life?' I tried explaining it to them. They had it in their minds that he'd done nothing wrong.

"Why shouldn't I file charges?" Kotulak continued. "If someone assaulted you, would you file charges? I was made to feel the bad one. . . . I couldn't even talk on the wall phone without one of them listening to my conversations."

Because of what she considered harassment, Kotulak moved to the second floor. Her grades plummeted because of the emotional effects of the incident, and as a result her chances for entering nursing school were damaged.

Meanwhile, Old Dominion brought disciplinary proceedings against Souther. Virtually all of Souther's teachers wrote letters or testified on his behalf before the court and the Old Dominion University Student Conduct Committee, a joint faculty and student group. Stanley R. Pliska, a history professor, said that while Souther was in his American history class he found him to be a "[d]iligent student, mature in his conduct, and mature in the questions he asked. His attendance was excellent, his grade in the course was an A, and his conduct on campus, to the best of my memory and observation, was always gentlemanly."

Dr. Mihalap, one of Souther's two Russian teachers, said of his student, "I have known Mr. Souther both in the classroom and socially for almost two years. I find no flaw in his character. He is an honest man, a good student, a reliable person."

John Fahey, his adviser, said, "He has an easygoing rapport with other students. There is a tendency for them to joke and kid one another, no more than I observed in previous classes. . . . It would be a tragic loss if Mr. Souther does not continue in Russian."

But Frederick E. Talbott, the adviser to the *Mace & Crown*, the school newspaper, took Kotulak's side. Having been introduced to her by another teacher, Talbott spent several days consulting with her. He worked with Response, the local center that helps rape victims. After looking at the mark on her neck, Talbott decided the whole matter was shocking.

"Everyone treated it like it was cute," he said. "At this university, we don't tolerate harassment. This was an attack."[110]

The university suspended Souther for the following semester, and he lost credit for the courses he had already taken during the spring semester.

Cindy ran into him on the campus parking lot just after the story appeared in the school paper.

"I was just goofing around," he said. "I went to the dorm and grabbed her and pretended to bite her in the neck. She freaked out. She was running around screaming."

Souther said he was afraid the incident might hurt his navy career, and he told Cindy he felt devastated. But Souther had devastated her, and now he was feeling sorry for himself. He showed no interest in how she was doing.

"What a selfish person," she thought to herself.[111]

Originally, Souther was charged with sexual battery, a misdemeanor. He was found guilty in General District Court of Norfolk and was sentenced to a six-month jail sentence that was suspended. He was also fined $250.

Souther appealed, and on June 7, 1984, he agreed to plead guilty to a charge of simple assault. While the charge carried the same penalties as sexual battery, the prosecutor decided that Souther's offense was not sexual in nature. Under Virginia law, simple assault means "any bodily hurt however slight, done to another, in an angry, rude, or vengeful manner."

At the request of Souther's lawyer, Judge Robert W. Stewart of the Circuit Court of Norfolk ordered a presentence report. The report was generally favorable. Souther had never been in trouble with the law and had performed well in the navy and in school. In addition, the judge reviewed a slew of favorable letters from Old Dominion faculty members. Finally, he took note of the fact that Old Dominion had already punished Souther by withholding all his credits for the current semester and suspending him for the following one.

What impressed the judge was that both sides agreed on what had happened. The question was how it was perceived. After all, a hickey in other circumstances is considered a sign of love. On the other hand, so is sexual intercourse. When it is performed without consent, it is considered rape. Souther claimed that what he had done was a foolish prank; Kotulak claimed she was violated. The problem lay in balancing the two competing perceptions.

Based on the favorable information he reviewed and the fact that Souther had not intended to hurt anyone, Judge Stewart reduced the charge to disorderly conduct on August 27, 1984. In the end, he decided that clearly there had been a general uproar in the dorm as a result of Souther's actions. Not only had Souther bitten Kotulak on the neck, but he had pursued her into her room twice without permission. Disorderly conduct is an all-inclusive charge covering all kinds of disturbances. The judge decided it neatly fit the incident. While it carries the same penalties as sexual battery and simple assault, disorderly conduct would not look as bad on Souther's record. He fined him one hundred dollars.[112]

14

I spit on the fact
that neither Homer nor Ovid
invented characters like us,
pock-marked with soot.
I know
the sun would dim, on seeing
the gold fields of our souls!

—VLADIMIR MAYAKOVSKY, "A Cloud
in Trousers"

ON JUNE 18, 1984, Souther began attending the Russian School at Norwich University in Vermont, a summer program for serious students of the Russian language. Set in idyllic rolling green hills near Northfield, the school requires each student to speak Russian at all times. The program includes Russian singing, dancing, drama, and cooking, along with Russian films, lectures, and concerts.[113]

Souther attended the school along with Klein and a handful of other students from Old Dominion's Russian Club. Soon, he had turned the two-hundred-student school into a rural version of *Animal House*. It was a measure of his ability to manipulate that he maintained good relations all the while with his teachers.

"He charmed the pants off them [his teachers at Norwich]," Klein said. "He really knew how to play to people. He knew what they wanted to see in him."

Souther would tone down his risqué comments with older, straitlaced Russian émigrés just enough to fall within the bounds of good taste.

"We would be talking with a teacher together, and he would say, 'Danine was busy last night. I saw her with another guy. How could she possibly have learned the structure of this irregular verb because she was studying about getting to know men?' It would imply something dirty. He would still be himself and curb himself only a little."[114]

Souther would drink with male Russian teachers and buy them Russian cognac.

"That's a really adept way to become friendly with a Russian, to bring a bottle of booze they like and have a good long heart-to-heart à la Dostoevsky about sex and death and love and life," Klein said. "He knew that, and he could exploit that."

Occasionally, he slipped girls dirty notes.

"You want *kaak?*" he wrote to Klein, referring to the Russian word for "how."

Souther took particular delight in tormenting Jon Berryman, a member of the Russian Club who had just become a born-again Christian. Berryman is pudgy, with blond, fluffy hair parted almost down the middle, as if he couldn't decide where to put the part. He has blue eyes and baby-soft skin.

Now that he had become religious, Berryman was trying to convert everyone in sight. Klein recalled that Souther—who had long since discarded religion—teased him about it mercilessly.

"Anything was fair game for Glenn. Jon never heard the end of abuse for being a Bible-thumping, born-again Baptist," she said.

Berryman, on the other hand, was convinced that Souther had chosen to pick on him because he thought he would tell

Souther's latest girlfriend back in Norfolk about his blossoming affairs at Norwich.

"He always had a string of girlfriends," Klein said. "They were always extremely serious relationships. It would be very passionate, then burn out. It would last for a month or more. When it ended, he wanted nothing to do with her. But in the beginning she was the woman of his destiny. He would rave about her. 'Exciting, beautiful, intellectual.' He always provided sexual details. He shared all of those with me, he shared them with everyone: 'She is passionate. A tiger. Couldn't get enough. Always ready.' "

If Klein ever began thinking that Souther would make a good boyfriend, she reminded herself of how fickle he was. Besides, she thought he was too skinny.[115] Souther weighed 145 pounds distributed over a five-foot eleven-inch frame. His body was pale and lean, lanky like a high school athlete's or a long-distance runner's. His shoulders were small for a grown man's. His arms did not bulge with muscles; they moved in simple unassuming curves. His stomach was tight. His legs were muscular and lean, with knobby knees sticking out. The dark hair on his chest contrasted with his white skin. From far away, the black hair on his chest and stomach was reminiscent of black paint splashed on a tie-dyed T-shirt.

Berryman took it upon himself to defend each girlfriend Souther discarded, always prefacing his remarks by saying, "I realize it's not really my business." When Souther broke up with Cindy, Berryman talked with Souther about it.

"Why did you just break up with her so suddenly?" he asked.[116]

"It just happened," Souther said.

Almost immediately after breaking up with Cindy, Souther had started going with another young woman—Dory. With

----

long brown hair, big brown eyes, and shapely legs, she was a knockout. Souther told Klein that Dory was the girl of his dreams, but by then Klein had become inured to such claims.

By the time he entered Norwich, Souther had tired of Dory.[117] Though she continued to live in his apartment back in Norfolk, he did not, according to Klein, even open her letters while he was in Vermont.

"I thought it was rather strange the way he could just end one relationship and go into another one," Berryman would explain later. "His attitude seemed rather selfish to me. That he could make someone feel like he really loved them for a long time, and then something would happen." The pattern had begun with Amy Rodenburg when Souther was fifteen. He was always looking for something better, for some kind of escape.

Souther regaled Klein with stories of Berryman's self-righteousness, not all of them true. For example, he told Klein that one afternoon Berryman had learned that his roommate was taking a shower with his girlfriend in the dorm bathroom. He broke into the bathroom, lifted the shower curtain, and began spouting verses from the Bible, according to Souther.

"You have sinned!" he shouted at the couple.[118]

The roommate gave him a black eye, and later Souther wrote an essay about Berryman and the roommate for one of his Russian classes. The teacher loved it and gave him an A.

"Is the story real?" the teacher wanted to know.

"Yes, and the star of the essay is standing right here," Souther said, pointing to a crimson Berryman—or so Souther told Klein.

It was a good story, but Souther had taken parts of true stories and embellished them. Berryman's roommate was having financial problems and had to leave school early. Berry-

man asked him to pay his share of the utilities—about forty
dollars—and he refused. At the same time, Berryman wanted
his share of the security deposit returned, so he took his roommate's textbooks and sold them. When the roommate found
out, he gave Berryman a black eye.[119]

And Berryman did object to the fact that his roommate was
sleeping with a girl. One morning as Berryman was leaving his
bedroom, he had encountered his roommate's blond, nubile
girlfriend wrapped in a towel, walking toward him from the
bathroom.

"I think people should wait until they're married to have
sex," Berryman would later pronounce. "I think you have to
be totally committed to each other. I mean, sex is not a game.
It's a serious commitment between two people and not something to be regarded lightly."

At the final school banquet in the community room, Souther
baited Berryman by saying God was dead. This was too much
for Berryman, who rose to the bait and called Souther a sinner.

"Oh, come on, Jon, you know you want to commit all those
sins, too," Souther said. "Just think of it! Imagine what it would
be like to have a real woman, Jon! But you can't, Jon, because
you're a virgin."

Boiling over with fury, Berryman threw a glass of wine at
Souther. Souther ducked, and the glass hit an elderly matriar-
chal school administrator. Despite his profane mouth, Souther
knew how to ingratiate himself with older people, and the administrator was no exception. Instead of blaming Souther, she
became furious at Berryman, who then tore after Souther, vow-
ing to kill him. Berryman finally left a note for Souther at his
door, swearing that he would make sure he spent eternity in
hell.[120]

Just before they went back to Norfolk, Souther formed a

----

hex out of toilet paper on the floor of Berryman's room. He placed Berryman's Bible in the center.

After such escapades, Souther invariably would say he was sorry, then offer to shake hands. He would then open his fly, snake his arm into his pants, and shake hands through the opening.

Invariably when Berryman would call Souther back in Norfolk, Souther would put down the phone and perform some chore in his apartment while Berryman continued to talk, oblivious of the fact that no one was listening. When he did it in Klein's presence, she would hover over him, urging him to get back on the phone before Berryman realized no one was listening to him.

Still, Berryman and Souther remained friends. Despite his proclaimed misgivings about him, Berryman looked up to Souther and wanted to be part of his crowd. For his part, when Berryman transferred to the University of Illinois in Chicago, Souther arranged with his mother to let Berryman stay in his grandmother's vacant house rent-free.

In retrospect, Berryman decided that they never had a deep friendship. While he testified on Souther's behalf before the Old Dominion student conduct committee, Berryman later decided the biting incident was Souther's fault after all.[121]

"When I got a chance to see him for what he really was, I couldn't blame the girl [for pressing charges]," he said. "Glenn was really a very self-seeking person. There wasn't an altruistic bone in his body."

Berryman would later say that Souther's profane mouth was responsible at least in part for his own decision to turn to religion.

"He would take a phrase and turn it into something dirty and disgusting with some sexual innuendo," he said. "He definitely had some kind of hostility toward religion. He would make up stories about nuns and priests, and it would be tied up with sexual innuendo and the idea that these people fool around."

At a Russian Club party at Berryman's house, Souther had pulled down his pants. Another night, Berryman was out with Souther in the Ghent section of Norfolk when Souther began running through the neighborhood with his pants down.

"I think that if anything made me start thinking about God and morality, it was Glenn," Berryman later said. "If he said anything, it was disgusting. He had no morals at all."[122]

But this was hindsight. Like the rest of Souther's friends, Berryman enjoyed Souther, his mild flouting of authority, and the way he turned any gathering into a memorable event.

One Friday night while attending Norwich, Souther, Mitchell J. Stout, another Norwich student from Old Dominion, and several others were driving back from Montpelier after dinner. They were stopped at a police roadblock; a police officer asked if anyone had been drinking.

"No. I had one drink with dinner," said Stout, who was driving.

"Yeah, I've been drinking. Yeah, how's it going?" Souther said from the backseat.[123]

The next day, Souther walked up to a female friend of Stout's who was wearing a short-cut T-shirt.

"She didn't really have a stomach worth showing off. He said, 'You really shouldn't wear that. You don't really look good in that.' She was pissed off and ignored him."

Despite the antics, Souther got B's at Norwich and received commendations for his extracurricular activities, including his work as school photographer. He acted in *A Bear*, a play by Anton Chekhov.

"He was very good," Dr. Issa R. Zauber, one of his Russian teachers, recalled. She liked him.[124] "He was always hugging, kissing, or joking. He was that kind of person," she said.

Another Russian teacher was charmed by Souther's interest in her two-year-old son. Souther carried the child on his shoulders and played with him on the verdant lawns. The boy called Souther "Dya-dya Gleb"—in Russian, "Uncle Gleb."

15

Have you seen
a dog lick the hand that thrashed it?!
—VLADIMIR MAYAKOVSKY, "A Cloud
in Trousers"

HAVING BEEN SUSPENDED from college for the fall semester, Souther managed to get a full-time job working for the
navy public affairs office. In that position, he had access only
to low-level intelligence that would be of interest to the
Soviets—operational, material, and personnel information,
photos of new weapons and ships, and reports on deficiencies
or impending changes.

Soon that would change. Just after he returned to Norfolk
from Vermont in late summer of 1984, his security clearance
was upgraded to top secret after a one-year DIS investigation.
In addition, he was cleared for access to sensitive compartmented information (SCI). Specifically, he was allowed access
to both SIGINT and PHOTINT intelligence, known as SI/TK.
SIGINT, or signals intelligence, derives from electromagnetic
sources, such as interception of communications or telemetry.

PHOTINT is intelligence obtained through photography or imaging, usually by spy satellites.

In December 1984, Souther was assigned to FICEURLANT, one of the most sensitive posts in the U.S. military. Souther was amazed at his luck.

Known as the FIC, the facility is the navy's Fleet Intelligence Center for Europe and the Atlantic. Reduced to its simplest terms, intelligence means finding out about the other side. Without intelligence, the military would not know where to drop its bombs or deploy its missiles. Nor would it know what strategies the other side has developed for penetrating its defenses. FICEURLANT receives and furnishes what is known as finished intelligence to naval components covering half the world. Finished intelligence is information that has been processed and analyzed and is ready to be used for combat purposes by ships, planes, and aircraft carriers.

FICEURLANT provides intelligence to the U.S. Atlantic Fleet, which includes both the Atlantic Fleet and U.S. naval forces in Europe. This area includes the Mediterranean, Caribbean, the west coast of Africa, the east coast of South America, the Black and Baltic seas, and half the Soviet Union. It includes both the navy's Sixth Fleet and the Second Fleet, which coordinates with NATO forces.

The center's most important function is preparing mission-planning kits or target folders for use by pilots who deliver nuclear and conventional bombs. These kits contain aerial or satellite photos of targets, maps, charts, and other information, including coordinates, needed to find and destroy a target. The folders also pinpoint escape routes for pilots once they have dropped their bombs. According to navy operational plans, pilots are to use certain corridors so they may return to the United States without being shot down by their own forces.

The second most important function of the facility is determining the enemy's "order of battle," military jargon for the enemy's capability. To obtain the information, the facility receives and prepares reconnaissance photography for intelligence on possible enemy concentrations; biographical information on foreign military and political figures; studies on amphibious, antisubmarine, antiair, submarine, and mine warfare; and country studies listing characteristics of interest to the navy.

In its massive computers, FICEURLANT stores the numbers, characteristics, and locations of Soviet ships, aircraft, submarines, land forces, and missiles. Included are such details as the ships' speeds, radii of action, armaments, effective ranges, electronic equipment, and defenses; the position, armament, equipment, and strength of land forces; and the ranges, locations, control systems, minimum elevation angles, susceptibility to countermeasures, rates of fire, and material conditions of missile batteries. Information on Soviet nuclear capability, including types and numbers of weapons and methods of delivery, is also stored here, along with a description of the Soviets' general policy concerning employment of nuclear weapons, terrain and weather factors that might favor or hinder nuclear operations, and the locations of Soviet stockpiles.[125]

Finally, the center keeps a computerized list of nuclear targets designated by the Defense Intelligence Agency for use by all the military. Known as the Single Integrated Operational Plan, or SIOP, the list is the ultimate nuclear war plan. It designates which targets shall be hit by planes, land-based missiles, or submarine-launched missiles. It also shows which military service—or which combination of them—is responsible for destroying each target.

All the intelligence agencies contribute to these studies and lists—the Central Intelligence Agency, the National Security Agency, and the Defense Intelligence Agency, as well as the various operating units within each navy fleet. Spy satellite photos come from satellites managed by the National Reconnaissance Office, in the Pentagon. As described in William E. Burrows's *Deep Black*, the satellites are diverse:

There have been low earth orbiters that could take standard photographs and then send them down in capsules whose parachutes were "snared" in midair by aircraft trailing special cables, and others that image in "real time"—as the action is taking place—and send what they see by simultaneous digital transmission. Above them, in the intermediate orbits between one thousand and 10,000 miles, still other space programs "ferret" Soviet, Chinese, and other nation's radars, making highly detailed measurements of their frequencies, ranges, power levels, and other operational characteristics. There are ocean reconnaissance satellites that travel in groups and follow the movement of foreign naval vessels. Still higher, along the 22,300-mile-high orbit known as geosynchronous because satellites sent there move in time with the earth to remain over fixed spots, there are still other spacecraft that monitor missile telemetry and intercept communication traffic, including microwave telephone conversations. Some satellites parked on this orbit use infrared sensors to watch for the telltale blasts that would signal a missile attack, while others are used to relay data from their intelligence-gathering cousins. Beyond geosynchronous, at 60,000 miles—about a quarter of the way to the moon—aged U.S. spacecraft named Vela stare down and register each double flash that signals a thermonuclear explosion. There are even satellites that travel in highly elliptical orbits disguised as data transmission types, but which really take the pulse of Soviet ABM radars so they can be nullified in the event of war.[126]

Requests for information from the satellites come from each of the intelligence and military agencies in the government.

The photos are first analyzed by the National Photo Interpretation Center in Building 213 of the Washington Navy Yard at First and M streets in Washington. NPIC designates which pictures to send to the military. Pictures for the navy go through the Naval Intelligence Support Center in Suitland, Maryland, and then to the FIC.

On his first day of work at the FIC, Souther drove to the compound where the commander of the U.S. Atlantic Fleet is based. Called CINCLANTFLT headquarters, the compound is marked by a blue sign on International Terminal Boulevard. Inside the compound, protected by an adjacent marine base, is FICEURLANT headquarters, a two-story brick building with no windows. On the roof is an oversize air-conditioning unit to cool the center's computers. Overall, the center looks like nothing so much as the pyramids of Giza.

At the entrance, Souther had to present a special identification card. The duty officer kept the card and gave him a coded badge that identified him as having access to the intelligence center. Besides a loading dock in back, the building has no other entrances. After signing in, Souther could either walk straight ahead through double doors to the first floor, or he could turn right through another door to a staircase leading to the second floor. Either set of doors had to be opened electronically by the duty officer.

In the southeast corner of the first floor was the photo lab where Souther worked most of the time. Pictures of beautiful girls taken by navy photographers on Virginia beaches adorned the walls. Here, Souther made enlargements and duplicate copies of spy satellite photos selected for special study or for use in the mission planning kits used by navy fighter pilots.

The photos processed by Souther were collected from all sources—satellites, aircraft, submarines, surface ships, radar, cameras on the ground, and other sensing devices including radiation-detection equipment. The spy satellite photos or images were taken with conventional photography and with other means such as radar or infrared.

Unlike intelligence from human spies, photography can permanently record operations at any given time, penetrate secure operations, present a bias-free portrait of an enemy's strength, and provide a record of changes over time. On the other hand, photos cannot capture intent, subjects cannot always be seen, and weather and light conditions can affect a photo's clarity. No target can be observed for an extended period of time, and vegetation, camouflage, or intervening terrain can conceal objects. Yet over time spy satellite photos have been so valuable that no major weapons system has been deployed by the Soviets without the United States first finding out about it.

In analyzing satellite photos, interpreters make measurements and compare them from date to date. Noticing something suspicious, they compare its appearance with reference books. One building may have smokestacks, which would suggest one type of facility. A rail line next to it may mean something else. Different industrial plants have different vats, types of containers, storage facilities, and smokestacks. Based on similar configurations in reference books, analysts may determine that the plant makes chemical or biological warfare components.

The photos that Souther processed showed the locations of Soviet facilities, the amounts and types of military equipment kept at specific locations, and numbers of available personnel. The photos pinpointed missile test sites, launch sites, and missile manufacturing complexes. They highlighted offshore gradients, reefs, and sandbars, as well as depths, beach gradients, cusps, and inlets. They showed physical features of the land such as soils, vegetation, use patterns, obstacles, exits, defenses, and indications of enemy military strength for use in amphibious operations. The photos helped determine the enemy's capability by revealing industrial facilities like aircraft and missile plants, petroleum refineries, electric power plants, and steel mills. By focusing on breakwaters, jetties, seawalls, harbor basins, and facilities for berthing, mechanical handling, storage, transportation, building, and repair, a trained eye could evaluate harbors, ports, and shipbuilding facilities. The photos revealed rail lines, depots, rolling stock, and train-marshaling yards. Terminal facilities for inland, coastal, and transoceanic shipping could be seen. Additionally, the photos identified highways, bridges, tunnels, aboveground pipelines, and pipeline terminals.

In analyzing the photographs, the interpreters looked for familiar shapes. Man-made objects such as hockey rinks and tennis courts are generally the same size and shape throughout the world. They are used as reliable criteria for establishing scale. Shadows provided clues to the shape and size of objects.

To help analyze the photos, interpreters used stereoscopy, digital processing, and color-coding techniques that enhance the results. By viewing two photographs of the same object made with successive, overlapping exposures, a photointerpreter can detect camouflage, details of terrain, and the results of military action. With digital processing, images can be compared by computer and stored easily for later retrieval. The material can be manipulated to present different angles of a ship or plane. This is of particular help to pilots who may approach targets from different angles. Using this method, analysts can superimpose data on existing photos, delete distracting images, or create fake pictures. They can read a license plate from a photo taken overhead. With radar and infrared, they can see into buildings and through clouds. Finally, with color-coding, they can impart a red tinge to one shade of gray

----

and a green tinge to another shade of gray. This greatly enhances their ability to perceive minute details of the photos.

Because of his work in the photo lab, Souther could easily make miniaturized or even microdot copies of spy satellite photos or other documents he obtained. Routinely, he was asked to make twenty-five copies of a key photograph for distribution to pilots, analysts, or other intelligence centers. Making an extra copy was as easy as pressing a button one more time.

While Souther's main workplace was in the photo lab, he had access to the entire building. Often, analysts called him into their offices for help on particular problems. Many of these offices contained even more sensitive material than the photo lab did. Indeed, for Souther the rest of the building presented a spy smorgasbord.

In the opposite corner from the photo lab was a library. It held classified reference books with intelligence estimates and country studies listing the characteristics of target areas. Along the north wall was the computer center containing most of the intelligence data used by the FIC. Next to the computer center were the print and graphics shops that produced mission planning kits.

The inner sanctum was upstairs. Along the south wall on the second level was the order-of-battle corridor. Adjoining the corridor were individual offices of analysts who produced studies on particular subjects, such as Soviet naval ships or Soviet electronic equipment. The information from their studies was stored in computers and could be printed out to show the enemy's capability in any particular area. The same material eventually wound up in classified reference books disseminated to the fleets.

In the center of the top floor were the administrative offices—the offices of the commanding officer and executive officer, budget officer, and supply officer. Personnel records were also kept here.

Along the north wall were three vaults made of eight-inch-thick reinforced concrete. A magnetic switch alerted the duty officer if anyone opened a vault door without using the appropriate codes. Ultrasonic sensors and vibration sensors detected any attempt to break through the walls or doors. As a backup, motion detectors using transceivers pinpointed the location of anyone who was in the vaults without authorization. Finally, if anyone tried to push a hand or arm through a ventilating duct or to touch particular files or computer terminals in the vaults, an alarm would sound.[127]

In accordance with procedures for handling top-secret material, each document in the vaults was numbered and entered into the command's accountability register, along with a listing of the number of copies of the document and the disposition of each copy. A top-secret control officer checked the document when any pages were removed or changed. Documents could be destroyed only in the presence of two officials, and a record of the destruction was kept with their signatures. The documents could be distributed by hand only, with a record kept of each individual who received them. Copies could be made only with the approval of the originating agency or higher authority, and each copy had to be annotated to show its copy number.[128]

The vault in the northeast corner of the building contained the Single Integrated Operation Plan (SIOP), the list of all nuclear targets, including which services are responsible for hitting them. Inside the vault analysts produced mission planning kits for delivery of nuclear weapons. Through terminals in the vault, the analysts could retrieve information relating to each target, including coordinates, the type of target, its defenses, and alternate targets in case the planes could not achieve their objectives.

Next to the SIOP vault along the north wall was the Special Activities Office (SAO) vault, where spy satellite and signals intelligence was received, analyzed, and stored. The material was then used for mission planning kits and for planning conventional warfare operations by fleet commanders.

With a real-time monitor in the SAO vault, navy officers could watch a battle going on and see the enemy moving up forces. While the resolution was not as good as with a photo, navy officers peering at the television monitors could see if missiles had been launched, if a target had been destroyed, and whether or not additional action was needed to destroy the target.

A third vault adjacent to the SIOP vault contained DORA, a code word for information about the deployment of submarine-based missiles. In this vault analysts could obtain the current locations of submarines, one of the most carefully guarded secrets in the military. To preserve the secrecy of the vaults, each one used a separate computer system. Next to the DORA vault in the northeast corner of the top floor was a room where material was prepared for marine amphibious landings and helicopter support.

During the weekend, when Souther had reserve duty, most of the offices were empty and could be entered at will. He could enter others—like the DORA vault—only when they were occupied. He could either smuggle the documents out or make photographic copies that could be more easily concealed. In any case, because of the high level of his security clearance, he was trusted. Like the rest of FICEURLANT's three hundred employees, Souther was not searched when he left for the day.

"If you had the ticket [clearances that Souther had], you could learn anything that went on there. Support elements [like photographers] deal with everybody in the organization, just like computer people. They don't do just one job. They support everybody dealing with intelligence. They have contact with everybody in the shop," said a former navy officer who worked at the FIC.[129]

It was a spy's dream come true.

16

I,
mocked by my contemporaries
like a prolonged
dirty joke,
I perceive whom no one sees,
crossing the mountains of time.

—VLADIMIR MAYAKOVSKY, "A Cloud
in Trousers"

NOW THAT Souther had unparalleled access to U.S. military secrets, he plunged into work at Old Dominion even harder. As he once explained to Di Palma, doing a good job was the best way to throw off suspicion.

In addition to his Russian studies, Souther became intensely interested in public speaking, eventually declaring it as a second major. He developed a close relationship with Frances J. Hassencahl, assistant professor of speech communication. The first course Souther took with Hassencahl was Communication Between the Sexes—an examination of differences in communication based on sex and how these differences show up in verbal and nonverbal behavior. It was then that he and the professor developed a bond based on his strong support of women's rights, their mutual love of "Doonesbury" cartoons, and their frank approach to the issues of the day.

If Hassencahl knew anything about Souther's tendency to

view women as tissue paper, discarding them after he used them, his charm diverted her attention.

"I'm a feminist," she said. "He did not see women as sex objects. He believed in equal rights."[130]

Souther worked hard in Hassencahl's courses and was considered a bright student.

"Basically he had the ability to understand and remember and put back together communications. He wrote well and was able to synthesize material and pick out key points," she said.

If he liked attention and was a bit immature, Hassencahl did not consider him to be uncontrollable.

"He was fairly responsive to direction," she said. "He was very social but not excessively so."

With Hassencahl's encouragement, Souther competed in national public speaking contests and won several awards. On these trips, Souther would tease and cut up.

Theresa Fisher, who traveled with him to several of the tournaments, recalled that he was a supportive team player who always made her laugh. Like many of Souther's friends, she thought she had a special relationship with him.

"He was the type of person whom you really like or really thought was disgusting," she said. "A lot of people didn't like him but I liked him a lot. He was a unique person. I think he had a genuine concern for people. We had a close relationship. He would rarely open up and show his concern in public but he always encouraged everyone and kept the team morale up. Even though he was older than most of us, he would always ask for our support. When I had a free round, he would ask me to watch him and criticize him."

At a tournament in North Carolina, Fisher told Souther that she had been distracted during one round because a female judge had a cold and kept sneezing. Just then, the judge walked down the corridor in front of a crowd of other team members.

"Excuse me," Souther said to her, "do you know you have snot on your coat?"

The judge looked at her coat, saw there was nothing on it, and laughed along with everyone else.[131]

At another tournament, Souther was staying in the same hotel room with William N. Goodbar, the assistant coach of the team. Leaving Goodbar in his underwear to watch TV, Souther gave the key to the room to five girls, telling them there was a party going on. When they entered, Goodbar ran for cover.[132]

During a tournament in the South, several female students from Mississippi began making calls to students in their hotel rooms, asking if they wanted a "good time." Souther got one of the calls. Recognizing their voices, he called them back and pretended he was black.

"I have twelve and a half feet of throbbing pleasure," he told them.[133]

They quickly stopped.

After the tournament, Souther and several girls were driving back to Norfolk when the subject of conversation turned to French ticklers. One of the students said she was disgusted by the idea. At a service station, Souther bought some condoms from a dispenser and left the package in her briefcase, writing "Fred," the name of another teammate, on the box.

"I can't believe it," she said to Souther later. "Fred put this in my briefcase."

Unlike Hassencahl, Goodbar did not think Souther's antics were cute.

"He put his arms around everyone. I was not that type of person," Goodbar said.[134] "When he got to be too boisterous, I just said, 'Glenn, turn it off.'"

Despite the horseplay, Souther got A's in his speech courses and came close to winning a national award for public speaking. Meanwhile, he began to blossom in his Russian courses. At first, he had been getting C's and B-minuses. Then Fahey, his adviser and one of his Russian teachers, got him interested in a Russian essay contest. Souther wrote about Moscow's remarkable accessibility to the oceans, despite its being an inland city. When the essay, "Moscow, the Port of Five Seas," won first prize in a state contest run by the American Association of Slavic and East European Languages, he became more motivated in his other courses. Soon he was getting A's in Russian.[135]

It was during this time that he became mesmerized by Vladimir Mayakovsky, the poet of the Russian Revolution, who lived from 1893 to 1930. Mihalap, Souther's other Russian teacher, first got him interested.

Mihalap taught in a classroom with a long table in the center surrounded by chairs, a calendar in Russian on the wall. For his lunch, he brought sausages redolent of garlic, as if the Soviet Union had come to Norfolk. When walking down corridors, he would turn off lights in empty classrooms, muttering about the waste of electricity. He often spoke of his experiences as an interpreter in the German army, which he said he had joined to help liberate the Soviet Union from Stalin's rule during World War II. At other times, he would speak with an Irish accent, expecting everyone to laugh.

Like Souther, Mihalap enjoyed plays on words, forming seemingly unintended meanings. "Those poor slobs—I mean Slavs," he would say of the Soviets.

Souther's penchant for sexual innuendo did not bother him. After leaving the Soviet Union, Mihalap, then thirty-four, had been the oldest undergraduate at Georgetown University. He could empathize with Souther.

One day in class, Mihalap described Vladimir Mayakovsky, the Russian poet, as a dashing, crude, irreverent figure—very much like Souther. A Futurist, he was part of a movement of irreverent writers and poets who played on words and even invented their own words as a rebellion against existing literary traditions. For example, Mayakovsky would form a new word by combining two other words—very similar to Souther's penchant for using double entendres. Because of this tendency, it was difficult to translate Mayakovsky's work into English.

"Mayakovsky was rambunctious. He was brash. He was extremely talented. He was a born rebel. He wanted a new system," Mihalap told the class.[136]

Yet ultimately, Mihalap pointed out, Mayakovsky was a tragic figure, a man who first identified with the goals of the revolution but later became disenchanted by the bureaucracy that it fed.

"At first he wanted to overthrow the czar and felt it would be a real reform," Mihalap said. "He was an idealist. He believed the workers should have equal rights and people should own everything under the supervision of the party. He did not anticipate actually enslaving people even more than before.

"He supported the system to the hilt but also criticized bureaucrats who hindered the development of the system," Mihalap continued. "He attacked ugliness in public behavior. He attacked peasants for their backwardness. He attacked unhygienic conditions. He was a one-man propaganda machine until he realized that he wouldn't be getting anywhere."

Once Lenin died and Stalin took over, "He felt a new rule of oppression had set in. He could not handle the oppression of the new government. There was nothing he could do because he helped bring it about. The only way he could protest it was by committing suicide," Mihalap said.

Mayakovsky was found with a bullet in his heart, a suicide note on his desk. At thirty-seven, he had become hateful to himself.

"He could no more tolerate what he helped to create. He had no choice. He was honest," Mihalap told the class.

Souther began collecting books on Mayakovsky, spending hundreds of dollars to obtain rare editions from the Victor P. Kamkin Bookstore in Rockville, Maryland. Ironically, when he showed other Russian Club members the collection, he would point out the poor quality of the Soviet binding and paper.

"Here are the country's finest gems," he would say, "and look how shabbily they are treated."[137]

Later, during an independent-study course Mihalap taught, he became even more deeply entranced by Mayakovsky's life. At a speech competition, he won honorable mention for his rendition of his favorite Mayakovsky poem, "A Cloud in Trousers." The poem includes a tortured appeal to his mother:

> Hello!
> Who's speaking?
> Mama?
> Mama!
> Your son is gloriously ill!
> Mama!
> His heart is on fire.

Mihalap believed a student could not understand a man like Mayakovsky without understanding the context of his times and environment. He talked with Souther extensively about the Russian revolution and the emotional upheavals of the Russian intelligentsia. As an émigré, Mihalap was a fervent anti-Communist, which he communicated to his class in no uncertain terms. Beyond the classroom, Mihalap socialized with Souther at Russian Club parties, where Mihalap played the balalaika and sang Russian songs. Despite their closeness, the teacher detected in Souther no sign of disloyalty toward the United States. Mihalap felt Souther understood the Russian soul—sorrowful, inured to oppression, but also ready to spring into revolt when pushed too far. Yet he also felt Souther was a patriotic American.

To Klein, it seemed Mayakovsky and Souther were one and the same. They had the same passion, the same inner rage, the same penchant for saying shocking things that outraged people, and the same unquenched yearning for love and attention.

Mayakovsky fell in love with Lili Brik, who openly carried on an affair with him for fifteen years while she was married. At the same time, both had many other affairs.

"Countless numbers of people were devoted to him, loved him," Brik said after Mayakovsky's death, "but they were all a drop in the ocean for a man who had 'an insatiable thief in his soul,' who needed the people who didn't read him to read him, the person who hadn't come to come, the one who he felt didn't love him to love him."[138]

17

I am where pain is—everywhere;
on each drop of the tear-flow
I have nailed myself on the cross.
Nothing is left to forgive.
I've cauterized the souls where
tenderness was bred.
It was harder than taking
a thousand Bastilles!

—VLADIMIR MAYAKOVSKY, "A Cloud
in Trousers"

ON MAY 20, 1985, the FBI arrested navy warrant officer John A. Walker, Jr., charging him with espionage. Because of the considerable navy presence there, Walker's arrest was particularly big news in Norfolk. A day after the arrest, Souther was sitting in Fahey's Russian class. Before the class started, several students brought up the case.

"They should string him up!" Souther said.[139]

As it turned out, Walker's arrest would have unforeseen consequences for Souther. But for now, Souther decided his arrest was a good time to prove his loyalty to the United States. The unlikely vehicle for that show of patriotism was Svetlana Sapozhnikov, another member of the Russian Club.

Sapozhnikov had emigrated from the Soviet Union with her mother and father in 1979. A manager in a Soviet factory, her father felt discriminated against because he was Jewish. Relatives who had already emigrated to the United States had written letters to the family saying they had reached the promised land.[140]

Sapozhnikov entered Old Dominion in the fall semester of 1984, majoring in Russian. Among the Russian students, there was always a debate about which teacher was better, Fahey or Mihalap. Each had his defenders and detractors, and Sapozhnikov was one of those who favored Fahey. She felt Mihalap discriminated against her because she was Russian, judging her not on what she knew but on how much she had learned. While she admitted there was a certain logic to that, she felt it was unfair that American students were getting A's while she—a native Russian speaker—was getting C's. Then, too, Mihalap felt classic Russian was the way the language was before he left. He would call himself a purist, while some students thought he was simply out of date. At times, he would mark a Russian word nonexistent when it had appeared in *Pravda* the week before.[141]

Nevertheless, soon after she began classes for the fall semester, she received a call in her dorm from Souther. Souther said he needed help in Russian, and he claimed Dr. Mihalap had suggested that she might be interested in tutoring him.

"How do I know who you are?" she asked.

Souther began naming other Russian language students.

"Okay, but you have to come to my dorm," she said.

"No, I can't do that."

"Why not?"

"I just can't."

"Then I can't meet you," she said.

"Let me think about it," he said.

Two hours later, Sapozhnikov heard a loud knocking on her door. Souther and a friend of his were standing there. She let them in, and they locked the door behind them. Sapozhnikov's roommate looked at them strangely. Souther gave Sapozhnikov a bottle of cheap wine and explained why he had been reluctant to come.

"I raped a girl, and I'm not allowed to come into the dormitories," he said in Russian.

"Excuse me, what do you mean?" she said.

"I raped a girl. Oh, don't worry. It was a misunderstanding."

"Well, that was good," she said.

"I was dating a girl, we broke up, and I saw her in the dorm. I pushed her down and bit her on the neck. She cried rape. They had a trial where they accused me. The Old Dominion newspaper printed the story but had to print a retraction because I was not guilty," he claimed.[142]

Sapozhnikov thought Souther's Russian was quite good. She didn't think he needed much help. Perhaps Souther had made up the story about Mihalap. Indeed, she couldn't figure out why he had come. He never brought up the subject of tutoring. When he left, he took the wine with him. Then her roommate sprayed their room with air freshener because she thought Souther's friend smelled bad.

The following semester, Souther and Sapozhnikov had Mihalap for the same class. The classroom was in front of a women's bathroom. As they were leaving class on the first day, Souther saw a woman walk into the bathroom, and he pretended to follow her. Then, when they crowded into the elevator, a female student asked if Souther would press "3" for her.

"Didn't your mother teach you to do things for yourself?" he yelled.

By 1985, Lana, as Sapozhnikov was called, had become president of the Russian Club, a tribute to her ability to cajole students into helping to raise money without seeming to be bossy.

She always referred to the other members of the club as her "associates."

Despite her popularity, many of the Russian Club members thought she was overly flirtatious. Lana stood five feet, three inches tall, had a 34–21–34 figure, and tended to wear tight black miniskirts or tight black pants, revealing halter tops, and boots. She wore bright red jewelry that accentuated her sparkling blue eyes, frosted lips, and dark, shoulder-length hair.

At Russian Club parties she would come on to guests, then back off.

"I was a tease," she would later say. "I would act very friendly to people. I found the company of men preferable to women. I was very nice. I would say, 'If you have the time, you can buy.' They would think I wanted to see them."[143]

In fact, Lana had had only two boyfriends. Because she became drunk on a glass of wine, she never even drank. She came to realize that her vampishness was a way of compensating for the fact that she kept losing friends because she had moved so many times.

"Instead of getting hurt again, I guess I wanted to have a lot of friends on a shallow level," she said. "That's one reason I acted like that."

Because she came on so strong, Souther mistrusted her. Occasionally when she met new classmates, she would explain that she was from the Soviet Union.

"Oh, a Commie!" they would say.

"Yeah, I'm a spy," she would joke back.

The repartee gave Souther an idea. He would report that Sapozhnikov had tried to recruit him to spy for the Soviets. The little show of loyalty would put to rest any suspicions that might be developing about him. The same ploy was used by Karl F. Koecher, a Czech intelligence service officer who became a mole in the CIA. By reporting to the FBI a nonexistent attempt by the other side to recruit him, he enhanced his own standing as a patriotic American.[144]

Nothing came of Souther's report, at least not at first. But later it would cause trouble for Lana.

18

And when,
with rebellion
his advent announcing,
you step to meet the saviour—
then I
shall root up my soul;
I'll trample it hard
till it spreads
in blood; and I offer you this banner.

—VLADIMIR MAYAKOVSKY, "A Cloud
  in Trousers"

JUST WEEKS after Souther reported that Sapozhnikov had approached him to be a spy for the Soviets, Cindy, his former girlfriend, saw the movie *The Falcon and the Snowman* at a local theater in Norfolk. Cindy had not been particularly interested in seeing the film. It was her current boyfriend who had wanted to go.

Cindy was stunned by what she saw. Based on the book by Robert Lindsey, the movie portrayed the espionage cases of Christopher J. Boyce and his friend Andrew Daulton Lee. The two were arrested in January 1977 for selling to KGB agents in Mexico City classified code material used to transmit photos from the Rhyolite surveillance satellite.

The similarities to the Souther case were striking. Boyce held a relatively low-level, low-paid position with TRW Inc., a CIA contractor for the spy satellite program. He gave secret material to Lee, a drug addict, who sold it to the Soviets and shared the proceeds with Boyce.

Like Souther, Boyce was young and extremely bright. Like Souther, he had been active in his church as a child, even serving as an altar boy. And like Souther, he hated the United States and the American way of life. Thus his motives for spying—like Souther's—were more ideological and emotional than monetary. Indeed, there seemed to be a connection between Boyce's attitude toward his country and his resentment of his father. Boyce considered his father—a retired FBI agent—to be an unregenerate capitalist.

As Cindy watched the movie, her mind kept replaying her experiences with Souther—his hatred of his father, his resentment of the intelligence agencies, even his relatively low salary from the government.

> BOYCE: Every day I get these misrouted cables. Details of CIA covert action that have nothing to do with national security.... It's incredible.
> LEE: Now how much are they paying you down there, or is that some big secret, too?
> BOYCE: $140 a week before taxes.
> BOYCE'S FATHER TO BOYCE: Do you really resent me as much as you want me to think you do?[145]

The most startling similarities were in the spy techniques, known as tradecraft. The details were burned into Cindy's memory—dead drops, large sums of cash, meetings in foreign countries. Despite the fact that Boyce was getting incredibly valuable material, the KGB seemed to be thinking in the long term. His control officer suggested that he obtain training in Russian affairs and get a job higher in the intelligence establishment, just as the Soviets had suggested to Souther.

Cindy sat transfixed as the movie continued:

> LEE TO KGB OFFICER: American spy satellites. I can get you all the information you want to know about them.
> KGB OFFICER: When you have something for me, make an "X" one meter above the sidewalk. . . .
> KGB OFFICER: For $6,ooo, please sign.
> KGB OFFICER: You should consider majoring in Russian affairs . . . and then, think very seriously about applying for a job in the State Department or CIA.
> KGB OFFICER: You can't leave here tonight free of it all, any more than I can. Did you really think you could?

"This is it to a tee," Cindy thought to herself. "Even when we went to Italy, and he painted on the bridge. He did the same thing. Even the amounts of money . . . the way he was angry at the government . . . the way he left the country and used markings."[146]

Cindy's mind was reeling. She felt she could not confide in her current boyfriend. He might think she was crazy. Instead, she told her sister, Debbie. Almost from the beginning, Debbie had been suspicious of Souther because of the large amounts of money he always seemed to have. Sometimes, the two sisters double-dated, and Debbie's boyfriend had been particularly suspicious of Souther. He thought he was selling drugs.

One night, the boyfriend put it to Souther.

"I need some money. Could you get me into it?" he asked.[147]

Souther said he wasn't into drugs.

Debbie attended Old Dominion and lived a few blocks from Cindy. The next afternoon, Cindy visited her sister.

"I think I know what Glenn's involved in," Cindy told her. "I think he's involved in espionage."

"Yeah, [her boyfriend] and I had that figured out all along," Debbie said. "If it wasn't drugs or the Mafia, [he] figured out it was that."

That night, Cindy asked her friend Darcie Long to meet her at the Classroom, the pub across from Old Dominion.

"She told me she had seen *The Falcon and the Snowman*," Long said later. "She was real scared and nervous because when they went to Italy, Glenn had done things like that—painting on walls, going to parks at night. She was not sure what to do. She didn't know whether to tell somebody, because she thought he was spying and she was with him and might be implicated."[148]

Long was amazed that Cindy had confided in her. When they had first met, she had thought of Cindy as being secretive and closed. She didn't like to talk about herself, didn't even like people to know that she was a karate expert. But lately, Cindy had opened up more, coincident with her interest in psychology. In addition, Cindy had been influenced by Long, who was just the opposite.

"Darcie is extremely open and very much in touch with her feelings," Cindy said. "I think I learned a lot from her. She would say, 'It makes me angry when you do this, so don't do that.' Or 'Every time you do this, I feel sad.'"

Because she didn't want her to clam up, Long purposely tried not to react to what Cindy was telling her about Souther. But Cindy took Long's blasé reaction to mean that Long did not believe her.

"I didn't have much of a reaction to her tale that he was a spy because I thought she wouldn't talk about it then," Long said. "I didn't think I had any advice to give her. I had no idea of which way she should go. Usually I have an opinion. I thought she would never tell me anything again if I made a big deal of it."

In fact, she said, "I believed her. I believe she does not jump to conclusions and is not a frivolous person. I didn't want to deal with it."

Later, Cindy would say that if anyone had encouraged her, she would have gone to the FBI immediately. Instead, she agonized over it. Suddenly she began noticing articles on espionage. When the *Reader's Digest* ran one, she noted similarities to Souther all over again.

Cindy felt guilty for not reporting it. At the same time, she kept talking herself out of it. For weeks, she went over how the conversation with the FBI would go.

"This is just your version. You don't know anything about espionage," she could hear the FBI agent saying.

She thought the FBI might accuse her of trying to get revenge and ruining Souther's career—indeed, his life—out of spite. Sometimes, she wondered herself about her motives.

"Would I be calling to get revenge because of what he did to me?" she thought to herself. "Or am I calling because I'm really looking out for the United States?

"If anybody had said, 'This is a serious crime, look out for your country,' I would have done that. But if they find him innocent, and he becomes an officer, this is going to come up," she said. "I thought, 'You go see one movie and how can you be so sure?' It just drove me crazy. Should I or shouldn't I?"

Then, too, there was the fear that the FBI might try to implicate her.

"One of the reasons for not turning him in was they might think I was involved," she said. "I had no way of proving that I wasn't because I was on his trips and all."[149]

For the next year, Cindy would be tortured by indecision.

19

She came,
and thoughts of a madhouse
curtained my head in despair.

—VLADIMIR MAYAKOVSKY, "A Cloud
in Trousers"

IN MAY 1985, Souther attended his high school reunion in Cumberland, Maine. About fifty classmates showed up at the Verrillo Restaurant off Exit 8 on the Maine turnpike in Portland. Souther stayed at a nearby hotel with an attractive young woman who was not from Maine. He took pains to tell friends she was paying his bill. He confided he did not want his father to know he was in town.[150]

Souther spent much of his time with a former classmate who was then married. Afterward, he asked Bob Fitch, his closest friend in Cumberland, to pass a message to her about getting together. Fitch declined. Souther told Fitch he would write to him but never did. As he told Cindy when they were going together, he was not one to maintain ties. It was yet another facet of his manipulative nature.

That summer Souther attended the Russian School at Norwich for the second time. Before he left, he applied for Officer

137

Candidate School. By the time he got back to Norfolk, he learned that he had been rejected. It was a devastating blow, and he blamed it on the fact that he now had a police record because he had bitten Kotulak at Old Dominion.

During his navy career, Souther had received the "E" ribbon, a sea service award with two Bronze Stars, a good conduct award, and a navy unit commendation. His immediate supervisor at the naval air reserve public affairs office rated his performance outstanding, and the commanding officer of the naval air reserve in Norfolk cited him for his performance.[151] On the surface, his performance should have been enough to get him into OCS. On the other hand, his penchant for pranks and profanity, while at times endearing, did not help. Moreover, he faced stiff competition that year. When the Naval Investigative Service later asked the admissions officers, they could not recall any single reason for rejecting him.

Meanwhile, Jeffrey Smallwood, the navy lieutenant who was married to Di Palma's sister, had been transferred to Rota, Spain, where the navy maintains its Fleet Ocean Surveillance Information Facility. Known as FOSIF ROTA, it provides direct operational intelligence to the commander of the Sixth Fleet and the units under his control.

Having originally pooh-poohed Di Palma's allegation that Souther was working for the Soviets, Smallwood was having second thoughts. The details of the Walker case made him wonder if Souther might be a spy after all. In particular, he had heard that the FBI finally cracked the case when Walker's former wife called the Bureau. He had also heard through Di Palma's other brother-in-law that Souther had returned to Italy without letting Di Palma know he was there. What if Souther really was a spy? Smallwood would be blamed for having let him get away.

In September 1985, Smallwood reported his suspicions to

138

the NIS office in Rota. However, the NIS assumed that the matter had already been looked into in Gaeta nearly three years earlier. The NIS office accorded it very low priority. Rather than suggesting an investigation, the office sent an "information report" to the Norfolk office of the NIS. Under NIS procedures, this left to the discretion of the local office whether the report should be pursued.

After determining that Souther was in the naval reserve, the NIS sent the report to the Norfolk office of the FBI. Since Souther was now considered a civilian, the FBI had jurisdiction over him. Based on the material it received, the FBI assumed that the allegation had been checked out by the NIS in January 1983. According to the NIS report, no basis for the allegation could be found. What the report did not say was that Greg Scovel, the NIS agent in Gaeta, had not even asked Di Palma why she thought Souther was working for the Soviets, much less investigated the allegation. Thus the FBI's Norfolk office —the same one that had aggressively pursued the Walker case, leading to his arrest—put the Souther case on the back burner.

It would be eight months before the Bureau finally took any action.

20

Maria! Maria! Maria!
Let me in, Maria!
I can't suffer the streets!
You won't?
You'd rather wait
until my cheeks cave in,
until, pawed by everyone,
I arrive,
stale,
toothlessly mumbling
that today I am
"amazingly honest."

—VLADIMIR MAYAKOVSKY, "A Cloud
in Trousers"

BY NOW, Souther had progressed from Cindy to Dory to Marcia to a Jewish girl whose parents owned an ice cream store in the Ghent section of Norfolk. To Danine Klein, the fact that the girl was eighteen meant Souther was going a little too far, but she didn't say anything.

"He said she couldn't get enough," Klein said. "He said, 'Jewish women must be incredible. She's wearing me out.'"

At the same time, Souther kept up his platonic friendships. Besides Klein, one of his closet female friends was E. King Butterworth. Known as King, Butterworth is very self-contained, controlled, and unemotional, with pretty, big brown eyes and long brown hair. She met Souther in one of Fahey's Russian classes.

In the first day of class, Butterworth turned around to talk to a friend, and Souther said to her, "Turn around and shut up."[152] Butterworth decided she liked the fact that someone in class would not be dry and serious.

Not long after that, Souther and Butterworth were sitting at a bar across from Old Dominion drinking beer. Butterworth mentioned that she had never been to Chicago and would like to visit it sometime.

"Let's go tomorrow," Souther said.

Butterworth thought he was kidding. He wasn't. By then, Souther's mother and stepfather had moved to Rockford, Illinois, eighty miles northeast of Chicago. Souther said they could drive there the next morning in Butterworth's old Grenada.

On the way, Souther talked about Mayakovsky, comparing him with Serge Esenin, another Russian poet of the same era who also killed himself. Noting that Esenin had hanged himself while Mayakovsky shot himself, Souther said, "That [hanging] is the unromantic way to kill yourself. Esenin took the wimpy way out. A bullet is more heroic."

Later, Souther confided to Butterworth that from time to time he thought about how he would kill himself. Butterworth didn't think anything of it. He was always saying bizarre things.[153]

Souther's parents' house was on the southern edge of Rockford in an area of Baptist churches, farms, and large wooded lots. It was a ranch on Halverson Court with black shutters and a gravel driveway leading to a two-car garage. As they walked to the front door, Butterworth saw a red welcome sign with two ducks on the front door.

Inside were two huge Labrador retrievers and a Chihuahua. Souther's mother and stepfather, Joe and Shirley Wiergacz, enter the bigger dogs—Jet and Molly—in field training and tracking shows.

Butterworth liked Souther's mother and was surprised that

she put up with his antics. He was just as wild and lewd in front of his mother—whom he called by her first name—as he was with the Russian Club members.

Souther's brother, Tim, could never forget the time Souther made a double entendre referring to the male sex organ in front of his mother and his grandmother Swartz. After he repeated it, his grandmother caught on and said, "You're sick." But his mother just laughed.[154]

On the way back from Chicago, Butterworth mentioned that she was planning on visiting the Soviet Union that year along with Fahey and members of the Russian Club. Souther told her he couldn't go because he was in the navy.

"If I ever went, I would probably love it there," he said.

Butterworth thought the remark odd. But she dismissed it.

Butterworth was having a rough time adjusting to college, and she was grateful to Souther for helping her when she became depressed. He comforted her when she became disconsolate over losing a boyfriend.

"He was always around to help me out and cheer me up," she said.

Souther gave her a book of Mayakovsky poems, inscribing it in his careful, controlled handwriting:

King—This is just a little something (little, nothing by Mayakovsky is little, but great) to help put a smile in your heart. Please accept this from someone who considers himself one of your closest friends. Always, I'll be there for you. Glenn.

Ironically, Butterworth went on to work for the National Security Agency, along with Andrea McGill, another member of the Russian Club who was a close friend of Souther's. Both had been recruited through a program Fahey had started for his Russian students.

When Butterworth told Souther where she planned to

work, a pained expression came over his face, as if he didn't approve.

She was shocked. To herself, she thought, "Glenn, you're in the navy!"[155]

One day after class, Souther practiced reading Mayakovsky's "A Cloud in Trousers" to McGill and Mitchell J. Stout, another Russian Club member. Souther planned on reading the poem the next day in a speech class. As Souther read, he seemed transformed. Suddenly, the class clown had taken on all the bitterness and cynicism of Mayakovsky. He spat out each word, as if throwing flames. When he read the lines, "Mama!/His heart is on fire," it was as if Mayakovsky himself had come back to life. The contrast with Souther's normally jocular manner was so startling that McGill began to laugh.[156]

Souther looked surprised and stopped reading.

"Okay, go on," McGill said.

McGill had a second major in art, and Souther commissioned her to do a painting of Mayakovsky for his apartment. She did an abstract, with garish streaks of color.

Another of Souther's female friends from the Russian Club had just married a military man but suddenly began having affairs right and left. She described each escapade in great detail to Souther and Klein.

One day, she told them that she had met three men in a bar and had sex with all three at once. "My friend and I were at a bar, and these guys were really nice," she said. "We took them back to my place. My girlfriend at one point was downstairs with one of them. But I also had them at one time.

"Well, I couldn't believe what was happening," she continued. "One moment I was with this one, then this one came into the room, and it was wonderful. Then the other one who was downstairs came up, too."

Souther laughed about it.

"If you had just mentioned that you like that, I would have done it to you long ago," he told her. "Here, let me do it to you now."

But he also warned her that she could get diseases.

Souther almost never talked about his work with his friends from the Russian Club. Klein thought he was a photographer and never knew he was doing anything particularly secret.

"I asked him what he did," she said. "He didn't want to talk about it. He couldn't be swayed. He never boasted that he knew things that were secret."

One exception occurred during a sailing trip on Chesapeake Bay with Ebba R. Hierta, another member of the Russian Club, and her boyfriend. Souther always felt more comfortable on the water, and perhaps that made him relax more. He confided to her that he worked in naval intelligence, analyzing spy satellite photos.[157]

Hierta and her boyfriend would never forget the trip because Souther confronted two coast guard enlisted men as they neared Cape Charles, across the bay from Norfolk on Virginia's eastern shore.

In Russian, he shouted at them, "We come in peace, you ugly fools. Your mother is ugly, too. And she dresses you funny."

Although they did not understand what he was saying, they understood that he was trying to provoke them. They decided he was suspicious and boarded the boat, giving Hierta and her boyfriend a ticket for having old emergency flares.

Through a mutual friend from Souther's speech classes, Souther went on a blind date in September 1985 with Ann M. McCay, a speech therapist with a B.A. and an M.S. in education from Old Dominion. McCay was a well-proportioned brunette who had been married once before. As he had with previous girlfriends, Souther fell hopelessly in love with her.

"We were in a restaurant, and he was all over her—cuddling her, kissing her, smooching, tickling her," Klein said. "That is something you would do as a teenager with your date. It's one thing to exchange a chaste kiss. But he was all over her in the booth. I was sitting right in front of her. It was very immature."[158]

It was a measure of Souther's ability to change his behavior for the person he was with that Mihalap, having met McCay, was impressed that Souther did not seem to flaunt his success with women.

"One trait in him is that he would come [to Russian Club events] with a young lady, but he would never overemphasize 'This is my girl.' He sort of played it down," the Russian professor said. "He kept his relations with ladies to himself. I approved of that."

Unlike Souther, McCay was mature and level-headed. The members of the Russian Club wondered how she could put up with Souther's antics. Soon, she became part of the club, attending Russian Club meetings and helping out at fund-raisers or Russian Club parties. As treasurer of the club, Klein was always willing to declare a party a club function and allocate funds made by selling doughnuts toward a keg.

Each of Souther's parties had a different theme. One time it was imported cheese, and everyone had to bring some. Another time it was cheap beer; whoever brought the least expensive six-pack was the winner.

At a Halloween party given by Souther, one girl showed up with a papier-mâché penis on her head. Sapozhnikov, who was dressed as a witch, was being particularly provocative that night. She asked the girl with the penis how she had managed to do such a realistic job.

"I'm a nurse," she said.

"I posed for it," chimed in Souther, who wore a toga, a cross on his head.

Souther approached Julie Woodward, another member of the Russian Club who went on to work for NSA. Woodward was shy and didn't drink. When Souther came out with his sexual remarks, she would blush and say, "Gle*nn* . . ." At the party, he urged her to try a screwdriver. She loved it.[159]

As usual, everyone was speaking Russian. It was one reason Klein referred to the Russian Club members as a "bunch of misfits." Recently, she and Souther had met a Panamanian friend of Glenn's for drinks, and Souther had insisted on speaking Russian even though the friend did not understand it.

"Carlos can't understand Russian," Klein said to Souther.

"Well, then you translate for him," Souther said.

By the end of 1985, Souther had moved out of his apartment and moved in with Ann McCay, whose voice had already supplanted his on his answering machine. McCay's apartment was a condominium unit in a three-story brick building at 620 Olney Road, just down the street from Souther's. They bought a Siberian husky puppy, naming it Vladimir after Mayakovsky.

At the same time, Souther went off active duty in the reserves to concentrate on finishing his degree requirements. At first blush this would seem to indicate that the material he was getting for the Soviets was not very important. But the KGB routinely opts for losing a few months of espionage material in favor of the longer-range goal of planting a mole high up in U.S. intelligence. Souther had just spent two weeks working full-time at the FIC during the summer, which gave him plenty of opportunity to smuggle out material. Moreover, he still had access to the intelligence center during the five months he was off active duty. Later investigations by the FBI would conclude that he probably visited the intelligence center at odd times and

took classified materials with him even though he was not supposed to be working.

Certainly his remuneration remained the same. Not long
after they began living together McCay noticed envelopes stuffed
with $2,000 to $4,000 in cash in their apartment. When she
asked him where the money came from, he brushed her off,
saying he got it "black-marketing bananas" or "smuggling."[160]

21

Maria,
as you see—
my shoulders droop.

—VLADIMIR MAYAKOVSKY, "A Cloud
in Trousers"

HAVING SPENT the past year wondering whether she should tell the FBI about Souther, Cindy finally made up her mind. When visiting her parents one afternoon, she decided she would report him. Both her parents were out, and the house was quiet. In the living room she looked up the FBI's number. The nearest office was in Manassas. She dialed, ready to blurt out the words she had rehearsed so many times in her mind: "I think someone is involved in espionage. Who do I see about this?"[161]

There were four rings, and then she heard a recording:

"You have reached the Federal Bureau of Investigation in Manassas. There is no one in the office at this time." The recording instructed callers to leave a message or, in the event of an emergency, to call the FBI offices in Washington or Alexandria, Virginia.

Cindy put down the receiver. She was not about to leave a

148

message, and it certainly was no emergency. It was a weekday afternoon, yet the FBI could not spare anyone to answer the phone. She thought again about how the conversation would go.

"What makes you think this?" she could hear an FBI agent asking.

"Well, I saw *The Falcon and the Snowman.*"

Cindy could hear the agent laughing.

"You saw one movie and you think your boyfriend is involved?"

"Yeah."

"Well, we'll call you next year."

Nevertheless, two days later, Cindy screwed up her courage and tried the FBI number one more time. She got the same recording.

Having agonized over what to do for the better part of a year, Cindy decided fate had resolved the question for her.

"Well, it was meant to be," she thought to herself.

Meanwhile, having received from the NIS an "information report" about the possibility that Souther was involved in espionage, the FBI's Norfolk office was in no hurry to pursue the case. It appeared that the NIS had already checked out the allegation some four years earlier. The NIS report said no basis for the allegation could be found at the time. The only new information was that Jeffrey Smallwood, the navy lieutenant who had originally dismissed Di Palma's claim, had heard that John Walker's wife had tipped off the FBI to his activities. This had given him second thoughts about Di Palma's original allegation.

What the NIS report did not say was that Greg Scovel, the NIS agent Di Palma had confided in, had never asked her why she thought her husband was working for the Soviets, much less investigated the allegation. As a result, the information the FBI's Norfolk office had to go on was quite different from what it had in the Walker case.

That case began when Barbara Walker called the FBI's Boston office and said her former husband, a navy enlisted man, was a spy. An agent based in Hyannis, Massachusetts, with no experience in counterintelligence, interviewed her at her home. Because she was inebriated at the time, and because the details she gave made no sense to him, he dismissed the allegation as being unworthy of pursuit. However, unlike NIS agent Scovel, he wrote a report on his interview. After three months, it found its way to FBI agents experienced in counterintelligence matters—Phillip A. Parker, then deputy assistant FBI director for operations in the intelligence division, and Joseph R. Wolfinger, who was in charge of the counterintelligence squad in the Norfolk office.[167]

To them, the details Barbara Walker provided—accompanying her husband to drop film and pick up cash in the woods of northern Virginia—were like a multicolored road map. All routes led to the KGB.

Wolfinger assigned Robert W. Hunter, a crack investigator, as the agent in charge of the Walker case. With strong support from Parker at headquarters, the FBI's Norfolk office then mapped out a comprehensive strategy for catching Walker in the act of spying. The Bureau placed wiretaps on his Virginia Beach detective agency and his home in Norfolk, coincidentally some five miles northeast of Souther's apartment. Since Walker retired from the navy in 1976, he had continued to engage in spying by obtaining secret documents from his son, Michael, a sailor aboard the U.S.S. *Nimitz;* his brother, Arthur, a former submarine officer; and his friend Jerry A. Whitworth, a navy communications specialist.

This photograph ran with stories around the world reporting Souther's death and speculating that he had been a teenage mole for the KGB. (WIDE WORLD)

Souther stole America's nuclear war plans and top-secret spy satellite photos from FICEURLANT at the U.S. Navy base in Norfolk, Virginia.

At age six Souther
struck a soldierlike
pose near his home
in Munster, Indi-
ana.

When he was sixteen Souther
(*foreground*) went on a religious
retreat at Lake Geneva, Wiscon-
sin, with his church group.

Souther's first sweetheart was Amy
S. Rodenburg.

Souther graduated from Greely
High School in Cumberland,
Maine.

Souther met his wife, Patrizia Di Palma, on the isle of Capri. (RONALD KESSLER)

Souther took Cindy with him to Italy when he met with the KGB, then posed for this picture in her relatives' home near Pisa.

After picking up cash from the KGB in Rome, Souther met a nun on the train.

Souther was proud of Cindy's black belt in karate.

Souther fell for another navy photographer, Kelli Templeton.

Members of the Russian Club *(from the left:)* Andrea C. McGill, Souther, Danine D. Klein, an unidentified student, and Julie Zipperer assemble near an ice cream store in Norfolk's Ghent section.

Souther attended the Russian School of Norwich University in Vermont with Klein and Julie Woodward.

Souther took photos of friends, including Carolyn Weiser *(second from right)* and Cindy *(right)* in front of the "Little White House," their home in Norfolk. (ROBERT GRAHAM)

Souther attended the Russian School at Norwich University in Vermont with Andrea McGill *(to his left)*, another Russian Club member, and others.

Souther stashed cash from the KGB in cushions in his Ghent apartment. (RONALD KESSLER)

Souther was arrested in 1984 for biting an Old Dominion University student on the neck.

Ann McCay, Souther's fiancée, got a push from Souther and Danine Klein shortly before Souther disappeared in 1986.

Souther showed up on Soviet television to denounce the United States.

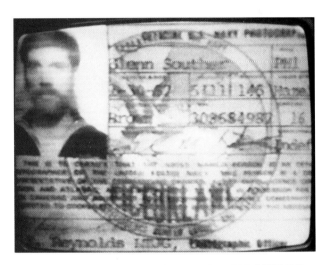

The Soviets showed Souther's FICEURLANT I.D. on television.

Roger L. Depue, former chief of the FBI's behavioral science unit, concluded Souther suffered from low self-esteem and a distant relationship with his father.

Under the supervision of John C. Wagner, the head of the Norfolk office, Wolfinger and Hunter came up with a strategy for following Walker if he drove to Washington to drop off secret material—a likely scenario since KGB agents posing as Soviet diplomats in the embassy are limited to a twenty-five-mile radius of Washington. When Walker got in his 1985 Chevrolet Astro Van on May 19, 1985, the agents were ready. Using a single-engine FBI plane and twenty FBI cars, they followed him northward to Maryland, where fifty agents and support personnel surrounded the area where Walker was checking out drop sites. They saw him leave documents for his Soviet support officer, and they arrested him with the KGB's instructions still in his hands.

In contrast, the Norfolk office treated the Souther allegation like dozens of tips that come into the office every month. Since he did not know the details of what Di Palma was prepared to say about Souther, Wolfinger assumed there were no credible details. He assigned the case to Richard (Butch) Holtz. A former probation officer, Holtz was experienced in counterintelligence but was occupied at the time with recruiting minority and female personnel within the Norfolk office.

Because the Souther case was seen as a low-priority investigation, the agent took his time looking into it. At first, the fact that Souther's address with the naval reserve was a post office box stymied them. To anyone familiar with the FBI's resources, such an excuse is laughable. When the FBI wants to find someone, it is quite capable of doing it. Eventually, through inquiries, Holtz found that Souther was attending Old Dominion.

If Holtz had realized how important the case was, he would have checked back through the NIS and interviewed Di Palma. He would have talked with Scovel, the NIS agent Di Palma approached. He also would have developed more background on Souther, his access to classified information, and his spending habits. Finally, he would have conducted surveillance on him to see if he could catch him in the act of spying.

He did none of this. Instead, he decided to interview him. The explanation, offered by a colleague, was "Sometimes an interview is all you have to go on." Yet the idea that a spy would simply confess because the FBI asked him to was naïve. Since 1975 more than fifty-six people have been prosecuted as a result of FBI espionage investigations. All but one of the prosecutions have resulted in convictions. FBI agents did not compile that impressive track record by showing their badges and asking suspects if they did it. As illustrated in the Walker case, the FBI as a rule carefully orchestrates its investigations.[163]

Planning is particularly vital in unraveling espionage cases because espionage is one of the most difficult crimes to prove. The evidence, in the form of documents, has usually already been flown to Moscow. Any accomplices are likely to be KGB agents who either have diplomatic immunity and cannot be arrested or are already back in Moscow. Thus it is vital that investigators find out as much as they can before confronting the suspect, making it more likely that he will tell all because he thinks the FBI knows all about his activities anyway.

Because the FBI realizes that it will usually get only one shot at interviewing a suspect, it takes another step before conducting an important interview. That step is to submit the case to the bureau's behavioral science unit at the FBI Academy in Quantico, Virginia. There, based on voluminous data from previous criminal cases, FBI agents trained in the behavioral sciences construct a psychological profile of the suspect and help develop a strategy for eliciting a confession.

The profiling program was developed in stages. Before 1972 the FBI trained new agents primarily in Justice Department and FBI offices in Washington. Only firearms training and other outdoor activities were conducted on the Marine Corps' sixty thousand wooded acres in Quantico, thirty-five miles south of Washington.[164] Because of the influence of then FBI director J. Edgar Hoover, Congress appropriated funds to construct a separate FBI Academy on the base. Consisting of low-slung, interconnected buildings, the academy resembled a small college campus. In addition to training new agents, the academy offered courses in law enforcement for state and local police officers. When the academy opened in 1972, it offered one course in behavioral sciences as applied to law enforcement. For the most part, the course—a potpourri of psychology, sociology, criminology, political science, and anthropology—was greeted with skepticism.

"Law-enforcement officers were not predisposed to having friendly relations and taking the suggestions of behavioral scientists," Roger L. Depue, who later became chief of the behavioral science unit, said. "They didn't want to hear a lot about theory. They didn't want to hear about the Oedipus complex. They wanted to hear what you do if some big son of a bitch is coming at you with a club, and you have nowhere to go, and how you can use words to cause that person to do what you want him to do. Consequently, police officers sat in the back of the room, leaning back with arms folded, saying, 'I dare you to teach me something.'"

But as they realized that the techniques being discussed might help them solve crimes, officers occasionally raised their hands and mentioned unsolved cases that had always troubled them.

"Law-enforcement officers have psychological baggage," Depue said. "I think all law-enforcement officers carry it. If you've ever worked a case, a kidnapping for instance, and you've done everything you could possibly do, and you sleep at your desk and you try as hard as you can with everything you possibly know, and the child is found killed anyway, you carry that around. It bothers you. I've known law-enforcement officers who are still working a case ten years after retiring."

As officers described the cases in class, other officers recalled cases they had worked on with similar characteristics. They would conduct brainstorming sessions, trying to analyze the similarities and the strategies that had worked best in previous cases. It wasn't long before officers were toting briefcases to the classes crammed with records of their unsolved cases. A separate course in applied criminology was formed to focus on the techniques being developed on an *ad hoc* basis. The classes actually solved cases that resulted in convictions.

What the classes found is that criminals, in effect, leave their signatures on the crime scene. These personal characteristics form patterns that can help identify the perpetrators and lead to their apprehension—if the scene is preserved and recorded well. For example, a person who is careful enough to dispose of a body in a river is usually an older person. If the body is dumped in a remote area, the killer is probably an outdoor person with a knowledge of the area. When the slashes on the victim's body are vicious and directed at the sex organs, the assailant usually knows the person. If there is no sign of forced entry and the assailant stayed around to have a snack after killing the victim, he probably lived in the neighborhood and knew the victim. In contrast, killers who don't feel comfortable in an apartment leave immediately.

To supplement this knowledge, the behavioral science unit began research projects to systematically amass data on certain types of crimes. Because it is the most serious crime, the academy began with assassinations. In conducting the research, FBI agents interviewed as many assassins and would-be assassins serving time in prison as possible, including Sirhan Sirhan, Sara Jane Moore, and Lynette (Squeaky) Fromme. The agents asked them questions covering fifty-seven pages and noted similarities and differences in the responses. They confirmed that assassins generally are unstable individuals looking for attention. In many cases, assassins keep diaries as a way of enhancing the importance of their acts. The agents also learned a lot about how assassins go about planning their crimes.

The unit went on to conduct research into serial killers and serial rapists. The assailants actually enjoyed sitting down with professionals who had conducted research on their crimes. It gave them a way of reliving what they had done. A clear pattern emerged. Most of the perpetrators lived a fantasy life that included enacting the types of crimes they had committed. With that understanding, the agents were able to develop profiles of suspects that police should be on the lookout for. Many times, these profiles conflicted with the leads police had gotten. Yet repeatedly, police and FBI agents have found the profiles were accurate, leading not only to apprehensions but to convictions.

For example, when police in a midwestern town found the mutilated torsos of two teenagers floating in a river in 1983, they identified them as a missing boy and girl, but they had no idea who had killed them. The behavioral science unit drew up a profile that said the killer was a male in his forties who knew the children. He probably led a macho life-style, wore western boots, often hunted and fished, and drove a four-wheel vehicle. He was self-employed, divorced several times, and had a minor criminal record.

Based on the profile, the police focused on the children's stepfather, who fit the description perfectly but had not previously been a suspect. They were able to develop enough additional information from witnesses to convict him of murder the following year.[165]

In addition to profiling criminals, the behavioral science unit began suggesting ways of trapping them. For example, the FBI's research found that killers carefully follow any details about their crime in the papers. The behavioral science unit would suggest planting stories in local papers pointing out that the anniversary of an unsolved crime was coming up. The story might also describe where the victim was buried. A killer reading the story might decide to visit the grave of his victim on the anniversary of the crime. By videotaping the scene, police have actually heard assailants confessing at the grave site. In some cases, they have enumerated details of the crime that no one else knew.

"They will even say, 'You bitch! The reason you're here is' such and such," Depue said.[166]

Police who have ignored the FBI's advice have done so to their sorrow. Not too long ago, police from an Illinois town lay out all day in a cemetery, hoping an assailant would show up. Because the weather was nasty, they finally gave up but left their video cameras running. Sure enough, the killer showed up. Because the police could not follow him, they do not know who he is.

"They have a videotape of a man, and they have no idea who he is. All they have is the videotape," Depue said.[167]

In espionage cases, there is usually no crime scene to analyze. Instead, the behavioral science unit tries to determine what kind of a person would engage in the crime and analyzes the personality of a suspect. Before doing that, the unit suggests ways of obtaining more information about the suspect—perhaps videotaping him as he performs his daily activities. In addition, the FBI may insinuate into his life an FBI agent posing as a bartender or businessman who becomes the suspect's friend. Wiretapping and electronic bugging may not only provide clues to the crime but help flesh out a suspect's personality as well. By making available to the suspect especially sensitive documents, the FBI may also provide bait inducing him to commit espionage.

Once a suspect is identified and background gathered on him, FBI agents from the behavioral science unit, led by Richard L. Ault, who specializes in espionage, sit down with the case agent and plan how best to confront the subject. The unit also develops a line of questioning that is most likely to elicit a confession. And it suggests the most appropriate time and place to do it.

For example, some suspects tend to enjoy staying up late and sleeping into the late morning. These "night people" are more likely to confess if interviewed at night, when their juices are flowing. The unit may suggest what day of the week to interview a suspect. Should the interview be in a hotel room or at FBI offices? Where should the subject sit? How should the agents be dressed? How should questions be phrased? These and more issues are addressed and resolved, based on previous experience with similar suspects, by the behavioral science unit, the agent in charge of the case, and superiors at headquarters.[168]

In the Souther case, none of this was done. No surveillance was conducted beforehand. No sensitive papers were wafted in front of him to see if he would take the bait. No informants were planted around him. And no long-range planning went into conducting the interview.

Because the case was considered only a preliminary investigation, no high-level approvals were required before an interview was conducted. Parker was told about it only in passing. Only a low-level headquarters official approved it. While Wagner gave his approval, he could not recall having done so. When it came to espionage, the Norfolk office of the FBI knew the ropes. No one in the FBI questioned that.

But everyone assumed that the NIS had done its homework on the case before it ever got to Norfolk.

On May 21, 1986, Holtz met with Souther, who had graduated from Old Dominion ten days earlier. He was again in the active naval reserve.

Because he had no details of the allegation, he could not pretend to know all about his spy activities. When confronting Karl Koecher, the Czech intelligence service officer who became a mole in the CIA, the FBI case agent told him, "I think we should establish one thing. We know who you are and what you've done since you arrived in this country. In other words, your association with the—as we would term it—opposition, hostile intelligence services. . . ." Koecher soon confessed to espionage, in part because the agents offered him immunity from prosecution.[169]

In the Souther case, Holtz and another agent merely tried to get a feel for what his responses would be if sensitive subjects were raised. Holtz asked him about Sapozhnikov, the member of the Russian Club who was an émigré from the Soviet Union. Had she made any more attempts to recruit him? Had he seen her lately?

Then Holtz asked about his Russian courses and why he was taking them. Normally, such questions would be irrelevant and could be considered harassment. But since Souther had a top-secret clearance, anything Souther did was subject to scrutiny.

Finally, he asked if he had had any contact with a "hostile intelligence service."

Predictably, Souther said, "No."

When Holtz asked if he would take a lie-detector test on the question, he said he would.

Holtz said he would get back to him about the lie-detector test. In fact, no lie-detector test had been planned. Nor was one requested. While Holtz was not totally satisfied with Souther's responses, he came away with no sense of urgency about investigating him.

The FBI had taken eight months to find and interview him, only to handle the questioning in a perfunctory manner.

22

Maria, do you want such a man?
Let me in, Maria!
With shuddering fingers I shall grip the
doorbell's iron throat!
Maria!

—VLADIMIR MAYAKOVSKY, "A Cloud
in Trousers"

ON JUNE 6, 1986, Souther attended a final gathering of his Russian Club friends. The occasion was a National Slavic Honor Society banquet at the home of Cathy Norton's parents in Virginia Beach.

Souther considered Cathy's mother to be an overbearing parent, pushing her child and bragging about her incessantly. When he got to her house, both faculty and students were dressed up, acting in the most genteel southern fashion. Cathy's mother welcomed everyone. When Souther saw that she was serving fruit punch, he said to Klein, "This will be a lot of fun, no alcohol."[170]

"Why don't you have a drink?" Cathy's mother said to Souther. "What would you like? We have soda, fruit punch."

"I'll have a beer," Souther said loudly.

Cathy's mother blinked.

"Well, I think we might have one," she said, and reluctantly got a Miller from the refrigerator.

"Now Cathy is going to play the harp," her mother said primly.

Cathy, dressed in a huge white dress, played a Simon and Garfunkel song. Klein thought it didn't sound right. When everyone applauded, Cathy's mother urged her to play some more. So Cathy played what sounded to Klein like the same song again.

Souther had driven to the party with Ann McCay and Klein. By now, Souther had proposed to McCay, and their wedding was set for July. They had even signed a contract to buy a condominium unit in a building under construction in Virginia Beach. McCay envisioned a lifetime of happiness with Souther.[171]

On the way home, Souther was in rare form, imitating Cathy's mother in a falsetto voice.

"Now we're going to gather around and watch while Cathy takes a shit," he said. "Everybody clap."

On the banquet table Cathy's mother had placed a cake that said, "Happy Birthday, A. S. Pushkin and Cathy," since Cathy's birthday and the birthday of the father of Russian literature were the same. This reminded Souther of the time Jon Berryman had thrown a birthday party for himself. Ostensibly inviting everyone to a Russian Club party, Berryman had bought himself a cake and announced, "Look, it's my birthday!"

Years later, Souther would tease him about it, and now he began comparing Cathy's mother to Berryman.

"Now we know why her mother said we could have the banquet at her house," he said.

Souther seemed to be acting the way he normally did— charming and obnoxious at the same time.[172] His adviser, Fahey, recalled that Souther asked him if he had heard the results of

----

the state essay contest in Russian. Souther had won the previous year, and he was excited about hearing the results this year. Every time he saw him, Souther asked him if he had heard yet, almost as if he expected to be leaving soon. Fahey told him he had not yet heard.

If Fahey thought Souther was acting normally, King Butterworth did not. In the past few weeks, she noticed that Souther had been cold and distant with her.

"I couldn't understand why. He was really different. He didn't seem to want to talk with me. That hurt my feelings," she said.[173]

The fact that he had just been interviewed by the FBI, and that Butterworth had accepted a job with NSA, almost certainly was behind it.

23

The paddocks of the streets run wild.
The fingers of the mob mark my neck.

—VLADIMIR MAYAKOVSKY, "A Cloud
in Trousers"

THE NEXT DAY Souther had lunch at the Classroom with
Frances Hassencahl, his speech communication teacher. He
seemed in good spirits; he said he had a job in the private sector
with Pentamation Enterprises Inc., a data processing and microfiche filming firm in Norfolk. Through another speech student, Souther had become friends with Michael G. Perrow and
Sharon K. Hodge, who worked for Pentamation. Both were
impressed by Souther's smooth approach, and Hodge admired
the fact that Souther felt he could breach social norms.

One morning a few months earlier, Souther had been having
breakfast at Shoney's Restaurant, a southern-style pancake
house, with Hodge and several other friends. Souther got up
from their table and addressed the other diners in a loud voice:

"Your attention, please! May I have your attention please?
I'd like to introduce you to my friend, Sharon."

Souther asked the waitress an obscene question and began

popping plastic straws by filling them with air, then crushing them quickly. The waitress didn't seem to mind. As they left, she said, "Good-bye, Sharon."

Shortly after that, Souther dropped a used condom down the back of one of Sharon's friends.

Just a few days before Souther's lunch with his professor, Thomas C. Watters of Pentamation had offered Souther a job as a salesman; he was to sell the firm's microfiche record-keeping services and a new software program that keeps track of hospital billing.

"He made a real good impression," Perrow said of Souther. "He got the job hands down over anyone else who applied."[174]

Whether he would have started work is another question. Most likely he had spent the past few weeks consulting with his Soviet contacts to see what he should do now that the FBI might be watching him. Despite his calm demeanor, he had probably agonized over whether he should tough it out or try to escape. If he were to escape, obtaining a new job would be a good cover. Souther was always talking about applying for a job with the Immigration and Naturalization Service or even working as a tour guide at the Hermitage Museum in Leningrad. Koecher, the Czech intelligence service officer, made similar claims about looking for a new job as a way of throwing off suspicion.

Now Souther told Hassencahl over lunch that his ex-wife had reported him for spying—probably an assumption on his part.

"She's crazy," he said.[175]

Souther said he thought his phone was tapped. He said he was going to Chicago the next day to see his mother. He then planned to fly to Italy to see his son, former wife, and brother-in-law.

"I'm going to talk to her face-to-face," he said. "I'm going to get it straightened out."

Souther said he expected to return in about a week. He would then have all his problems behind him and start a new job and a new life with Ann McCay.[176]

Meanwhile, he told McCay that if anything should happen to him, she should give his collection of Russian books to Old Dominion's library. He told her not to tell anyone he was going to Italy, since leaving the country without reporting it would be a violation of security rules.[177] He told Klein he was going to Washington for a job interview.

Souther flew to Chicago and told his mother he was going to look for a job there. But he said he was going first to Italy, where he had a problem to take care of. He said he would be back in a week. Souther did not elaborate, and his mother did not press him.[178]

Just before he left, Souther told his mother he would never forgive his stepfather for what he had done—apparently, he had hit him when he was younger.[179] He also told her he had been approached to take a lie-detector test and could not pass it if he took it. But he said he was not involved in espionage.[180] While Souther freely told his mother of his latest female conquests, he never told her about his double life.

Souther borrowed his mother's blue-and-silver Ford LTD for the ride to the airport. She told him he could leave it at the O'Hare parking lot. A friend from work would drive her there to pick it up.

On Monday, June 9, 1986, Souther bought a round-trip ticket to Rome on Alitalia flight 605. After a stop in Montreal, he arrived in Rome the following day. He never used the return ticket.

As an FBI agent involved in the investigation later pointed out, the Bureau may have mishandled the interview with Souther, but at least it had stopped his spying activities.

When Shirley Wiergacz picked up her car, she found

Souther had left behind his briefcase. In it were his navy papers and other personal documents. There was also a receipt showing he had bought a new briefcase.

His mother thought that was strange, but Souther was always doing strange things. When he did not come back in a week, she became frantic.

Wiergacz called Di Palma, who knew nothing about his whereabouts. Then she called Tim Souther, who had not even seen his brother when he came back to visit. She also called McCay in Norfolk.

McCay and Souther had agreed to meet Chris Philips and Andrea McGill, two of their friends from the Russian Club, at the Intermission, a bar in Norfolk, that Sunday. When they called the apartment, McCay said he had gone to Italy to visit his former wife and son. She said he hadn't shown up at the Norfolk airport. She had no idea what had happened to him.[181]

He had vanished.

24

Open up!
I'm hurt!

—VLADIMIR MAYAKOVSKY, "A Cloud
  in Trousers"

WHEN Souther did not show up for reserve duty the following weekend, the FBI was called in. At first, the Bureau assumed he had met with an accident or been the victim of foul play. He had not seemed particularly nervous or furtive when he was interviewed. The FBI still did not know what was behind Di Palma's allegation about him. Nor was there any record in Rome to show that he had left Italy. From the FBI's standpoint, he was a missing person.

As the FBI delved into the case, the most alarming aspect was the amount of sensitive information to which Souther had access. Even if he were not a spy, the disappearance of someone with that much top-secret information was enough to cause grave concern. It was reason enough for the FBI to be on the case.

A week after Souther was supposed to be back from Italy, the FBI called his mother. Her son's disappearance was like a

----

gaping wound. Largely because of the connection between Italy and the Mafia, she was convinced that Di Palma's family was torturing Souther or had already killed him.

"You have to find him," she told the agents.

She gave them as much information as she could, including names of former girlfriends. She also told Souther's brother, Tim, to cooperate. Later, Shirley Wiergacz would tell Tim she felt the FBI tricked her. They weren't just trying to find him; they were building a case against him.[182]

In fact, the FBI initially did not know if he was a spy. But some of the information provided by his family raised red flags. For example, when the FBI asked if Souther had extra money, Tim mentioned the $500 Souther went through during the week Tim visited him in Norfolk. He also told the agents about the $150 Souther loaned him and the four-hundred-dollar Italian watch Souther gave him. Based on his income from the reserves and the GI Bill, there was no way he could afford such items and pay for his tuition.

Wiergacz continued to call everyone she knew about her son's disappearance, hoping someone might have a clue to his whereabouts. The information she picked up was anything but reassuring.

When she first separated from Souther, Di Palma had intimated to her mother-in-law that her son might be involved in something illicit.

"Think what you want, but he is involved in something very bad," Di Palma had told her. She said he might be working for the Soviets.

Wiergacz had begun to cry and said it was not possible. "Maybe black-marketing," she said. "He would never betray his country."[183]

After his disappearance, Wiergacz called Di Palma and asked her what she thought. She said Souther had said he was going to see his former wife. Di Palma told her she didn't believe that story. He never came to see her or his son. She repeated that she thought he was a spy. Wiergacz said that could not be.

Wiergacz did not broach her suspicions about Di Palma's family's possible role in his disappearance. Di Palma would later ridicule the idea that her family would harm him.

"My mother always said, 'Whatever he did, I loved him like a son.' They [Souther's family] have a big imagination. They didn't want to accept the fact he was a spy," Di Palma said.

Wiergacz also called Cindy, his former girlfriend, who was even less reassuring.

"Glenn went to Italy, and he hasn't come back," she told Cindy. "You're the only one who's been to Italy with him that I know of. What did he do? Is there anything you know that would help find him?" she asked.[184]

"I don't know," Cindy said. "To be honest with you, I think he was involved in espionage."

"Now what makes you think that?" Wiergacz asked, pretending never to have heard of such an allegation. "That's pretty farfetched."

"I'm not an expert, but I saw the movie *The Falcon and the Snowman,* and everything that guy did, Glenn did. It hit me like a rock. My jaw dropped. That's what he's doing," Cindy told her.

A few days later, Wiergacz called Cindy again. She said she had since read *The Falcon and the Snowman.*

"That's not Glenn," she said.

Two weeks later, the FBI showed up unannounced at Cindy's parents' home, where she was then staying, and asked to interview her.

She told the agents how she had seen *The Falcon and the Snowman* and had called the FBI office but gotten a recording. Over the next three hours, she related how she had gone to

Italy with Souther and picked up $10,000 from "them"; how he had talked about picking up a "drop" of $7,000 in Washington; and how she went with him a second time to Italy, picking up more money and watching him spray paint on a bridge.[185]

Cindy mentioned the camera bag that he often carried, the secret writing, the disappearing paper, and the pill he said "they" would provide if he were caught. She told the agents that Souther said "they" told him to take Russian and get a higher-level job in intelligence. She said Souther had a gun. She also told the agents that Souther had said his grandfather had gotten him into what he was doing. In fact, there appeared to be no basis for the allegation. Souther's maternal grandfather had died in the early 1970s. His parental grandfather had no history of working in sensitive locations or favoring Communist causes.[186]

After two more visits, the agents asked if Cindy would take a lie-detector test in Washington. She was skeptical about whether such tests work but agreed to take one anyway. She was nervous, and the agents asked her to take a second one.

"They said they didn't believe me," she said. "There were a lot of inconsistencies. How could I prove I was not involved?"

Apparently trying to test Cindy's story, one agent said the amounts of money cited in *The Falcon and the Snowman* were not the same amounts Souther picked up. In fact, they were in the same range. The movie mentioned a sum of $6,000 given by the KGB to Lee. That compared with the sums of $7,000 and $10,000 Souther was getting.

At one point, an FBI polygraph operator asked her if she was aware that John Walker taught a private investigative course in Norfolk.

"No," she answered.

Apparently the agents were looking for some connection

with the Walker case, an issue that would later be explored at length.

"They were scaring me to death," Cindy said. "They said, 'You're going to be in trouble.' I started crying."

At one point, Cindy's father refused to let the agents in the house if they kept harassing his daughter.

"She's trying to help you," he said. "If you harass her, I don't want you coming in the house."

"We're just doing our job," an agent explained.

25

Maria—
you won't have me?
You won't have me!
Ha!

—VLADIMIR MAYAKOVSKY, "A Cloud
in Trousers"

By NOW, the FBI believed that Souther was indeed a spy—
one of the biggest in U.S. history. As the intelligence community
analyzed the material he had access to, many concluded that
perhaps he had done as much damage as Walker.

According to a senior intelligence official, it has to be assumed that Souther would have been able to obtain the most
valuable data in the FIC. That information, he said, would have
given the Soviets a wide window on U.S. intelligence.

By handing over codes to naval communications, Walker
enabled the Soviets to read daily message traffic, including naval
plans, ship locations, data on weapons, naval tactics, information on covert military and counterintelligence operations, and
emergency plans in the event of a nuclear war. If a war had
broken out, being able to read U.S. communications would have
been invaluable. Moreover, Walker's spy activities went back
twenty years. On the other hand, much of the information

Walker gave the Soviets access to was dated almost as soon as they received it. Moreover, it often did not include the kind of detail found in mission planning kits or SIOP lists of nuclear targets. This was information considered too sensitive to send electronically, which was the way the Soviets got their information from Walker's spy activities.

"The Walker material would give locations of a carrier today. So it's historical," a former high-ranking naval intelligence officer said. "Key lists [providing access to coded communications] can give you what happened in the past, but don't include a lot of future projections," he said. "Target planning and flight routes activated only in event of hostilities give you the future. That gives them quite a leg up in their defenses. It's more than just where to defend targets; it's also where to look for entry points and checkpoints. . . . In a sense, that probably is more damaging in the long run, although the ability to read radio communications is more damaging in the short run.[187]

"It's always fascinating to be able to read the other guy's radio message," he said, "but a lot of times, fascinating as it is, it doesn't give you anything you can do something with."

Generally, he said, the daily message traffic sent over classified circuits to a military command is of little strategic value.

"Each message has a purpose for somebody but a lot of it is just trash, particularly in the long run—daily reports, position reports, readiness reports," the former naval intelligence officer said.

More important, none of the information Walker provided gave away U.S. spy satellite capabilities. At first glance, that would seem to be a minor matter: most people know that the United States has satellites that can photograph anything below with great clarity, even through cloud cover. But like law-enforcement efforts to stamp out drugs, satellite surveillance has its limits.

If the Soviets know the swath, resolution, maneuverability, and targets of U.S. satellite reconnaissance, along with U.S. computer-enhancement techniques, they can build missile silos where they know the satellites will not be snooping—or save huge sums by eliminating camouflage at those facilities.

"Everybody knows they're up there. The question is, how good is the resolution and how often are they looking at a part of the world? How wide is the band? What is the coverage? There are only so many satellites up there," said a former navy analyst who worked at the FIC.[188]

"If you feel you won't get caught, you try something," he continued. "You could build something or fabricate a hidden bunker. When they're taking all these pictures, they're looking to see if something changed from the last time. To build a missile site or bunker, you're going to have to do some serious construction work. The question is, how fast can you do it, and how well can you disguise the tracks—the railroads, the roads, the materials?"

The United States sends aloft many satellites—looking like great metal-winged insects—whose true mission is unknown to the other side. Thus the photographs Souther had access to could enable the Soviets to pinpoint which satellites pose threats. With spy satellite programs costing billions of dollars, the stakes are enormous.

"It ought to be recognized that there is enormous potential breadth in the technological capabilities among different satellites," said Lincoln D. Faurer, who headed the National Security Agency from 1981 to 1985. "The only thing in common between one satellite and another is it's up there in space. After you've said that, everything else will be some differentiation among satellites—the nature of its technical capability, its orbital parameters, how often it sees the same place, whether it dwells or passes over quickly. All those things vary."[189]

While some details can be learned by observing the satellites, many features are designed to give the other side misinformation.

"There may be a bit of a problem deciding which satellite is a spy satellite," Faurer said. "In fact, we each think we know which are some of the spy satellites, but that doesn't mean we know what all of them are. You don't take countermeasures against unknown satellites."

"The reason for the great concern [about secrecy] is that almost every one of these satellites is capable of being frustrated by countermeasures," a former CIA official involved with spy satellites said. "If you're submitting something to photo surveillance and they find it out, they can frustrate that. It's always a question of tremendous losses—billions of dollars. If the other guy knows about it, he can turn it off for nothing [by changing its location]."[190]

While satellite secrets have been disclosed by others, none of the previous cases has been of the scope of the Souther case. Unlike Christopher Boyce and Andrew Daulton Lee, Souther had access to not just one U.S. spy satellite system but all of them. Unlike William P. Kampiles, the former CIA employee who gave the Soviets the technical manual to the KH-11 spy satellite, Souther could provide the actual results of spy satellite surveillance. According to Richard J. Kerr, deputy CIA director, a technical manual is like an "advertisement" which may or may not accurately foretell how a satellite will work in practice.[191]

By obtaining copies of spy satellite photos, Souther was able to let the Soviets know not only the resolution of U.S. spy satellite photos but also what the United States was interested in.

"In any situation, what the other side is interested in is very important, whether it's discovered by what they are taking pictures of or by a human source saying this is the intelligence priority," Faurer said. "It gives you all kinds of insight into what they deem important and are having trouble finding out some other way."

Thus the ability to steal spy satellite photos covertly goes to the very heart of U.S. defenses.

"The damage is in the eye of the beholder. From the intelligence standpoint, Souther is more damaging. From the navy's standpoint, Walker is. It means we have to revise our codes and equipment. In the Souther case, we're telling the other guy what we know about him," a former navy intelligence official with knowledge of the Souther case said.[192]

The fact that Souther only worked in the reserves made little difference.

"You can do a lot in a few hours if you know what you're doing," the official said.

Beyond that, the investigations turned up indications that Souther might have shown up at the FIC for extra work in between his regularly scheduled reserve stints. He told Chris Philips, his friend from the Russian Club, that the bottle of Rémy Martin VSOP they were sharing one night was a gift from his commanding officer for performing outstanding extra reserve duty.[193]

"Because of Souther and a few others, we could have lost a war with the Soviets," said a senior intelligence official with knowledge of the material Souther had.

While relations with the Soviets have since improved, the implications of what Souther did remain no less serious. For as long as the United States is faced with the need to defend itself against aggression by any country or group, it will require a military. And as long as it has a military, the United States will need to protect itself against penetration of military secrets and guard against surprise attack.

26

Then once again,
darkly and dully,
my heart I shall take,
with tears besprinkled,
and carry it,
like a dog
carries
to its kennel
a paw which a train ran over.

—VLADIMIR MAYAKOVSKY, "A Cloud
   in Trousers"

WHEN the FBI called Klein, she was shocked. For two weeks
she had been leaving messages on Souther's answering machine
and getting no calls back. She had no idea he'd disappeared.

The agents asked if she would meet them at their offices on
the eighth floor of Norfolk's federal building at 200 Granby
Mall.

Klein told the FBI that Souther always had plenty of cash
and lived above the standards of a typical college student. But
she said he had never given her any hint that he was spying.
In fact, she was quite sure he was a conservative when it came
to politics.

"I bet he would vote for Reagan," she said.

When the interview was over, Klein drove directly to the
apartment Souther shared with Ann McCay at 620 Olney Road.
McCay answered the door. To Klein, it looked as if McCay's

hair had gone half gray. She had bags under her eyes. She had lost a lot of weight and looked bony.[194]

"The FBI comes every day," she said. "I'm sure my phone is tapped. The house is probably bugged."

McCay told Klein that no one knew anything.

"I don't know anything. They don't know anything," she said, crying.

Patting their husky, Vladimir, she said, "I can't believe what your dad's done to me. Look at this. How can he do this? When is he going to come back to us?"[195]

Later, she told Mark J. Dickinson, a friend of Souther's from speech class, "I wish I knew he was dead; it would be easier."[196]

The FBI began interviewing Souther's teachers at Old Dominion, including Fahey, who said Souther had called him every few days until he left to find out if he had won the Russian essay contest. Souther never did find out that he had lost.

Then the FBI called on Sapozhnikov, the member of the Russian Club whom Souther had accused of trying to recruit him to the Soviet side. First, the agents were polite, but they quickly turned up the pressure.

"They would ask the same question, and I would say, 'Why are you asking me that again? I already told you the answer.' They would say, 'That's not what he [Souther] said.' I would say, 'I'm sorry that's not what he said. That's my recollection.' "[197]

The agents asked if Lana had ever dated Souther. She said she had not. They said he claimed he had been alone with her a lot.

"I said, 'I don't think I have ever been alone with him. If we were ever together, it was always in a group. Maybe it was walking to class and he said hi.' They said, 'That's not what he said.' "

When the agents said Souther told them she admitted to being a spy, she said that was true—but it was a joke. They were not so sure and accused her of being involved with Souther and passing information to him.

"I said, 'No, that's not true. I didn't even know that this was going on.' They said, 'Well, that's not what he said.' I said, 'Why don't you get him over here, and I'll tell him to his face? I'm telling you exactly what I know. I may not remember everything.' They turned around and said, 'We can't find him.' I said, 'Great. How am I going to prove myself right?' And they said, 'Well, why don't you take a polygraph test?' I said, 'Okay, I'll take a polygraph test. I'm not lying.'"

This time there was no delay in scheduling the test. Lana could not take it the next day because she was working, but the FBI arranged for her to take it the following day at the Washington field office.

"They asked my name, my background, whether I was a member of the Communist Party, if I knew him, whether I passed him information, whether I dated him," Lana said. "They wouldn't say what he told them. I would say, 'Where is he?' They said, 'We think he's hiding out in Italy.'"

In the end, the FBI told her she passed. But Lana considered it one of the more unpleasant experiences in her life.

Meanwhile, with leads provided by Souther's mother, the FBI located Kelli Templeton, the shapely navy photographer who was Souther's girlfriend before Cindy. Together with the NIS, FBI agents interviewed Templeton in Indianapolis, where she lives in an apartment with a boyfriend and works with retarded children. The agents learned very little. Templeton was not forthcoming about Souther's activities or her relationship with him.[198]

Later, after she had hired a lawyer, the agents interviewed her again. This time she related experiences very similar to Cindy's.

She told the agents she accompanied Souther to look for

cash hidden in logs or tree stumps at Cabin John Regional Park in Potomac, Maryland, where Souther said he was expecting to find $3,000 to $4,000. She went with him also to a park in the Dunn Loring, Virginia, area, to look for money. At various times, she saw him take down coded messages from a shortwave radio at 1:00 A.M., decipher messages using a code book or one-time pad, put colored tape on a phone booth, use microfilm concealed in a pen, and engage in countersurveillance techniques to throw off possible followers. This included such maneuvers as driving down a dead-end street and turning around, or speeding up to eighty miles per hour and then dropping down to twenty miles per hour.[199]

Templeton said she believed Souther's activities to be illegal, but claimed she was not sure he was spying. He never said he was working for the Soviets, but always referred to his benefactors as "they."

Unlike Cindy, Templeton was knowledgeable about espionage, since she had a security clearance from the navy. Such clearances entail receiving regular briefings about signs of spy activity, including such obvious tipoffs as receiving coded radio transmissions in the middle of the night, or concealing microfilm in a pen. At one point, Templeton did ask Souther if he was a spy, and he said no.

Templeton told the agents the reason she did not come forward during the first interview was fear of physical retribution and a desire to protect her family.

Templeton refused all requests for an interview for this book, saying she wanted to put the matter behind her. Therefore, her reasons for not reporting Souther earlier can only be guessed at.[200]

What is clear is that if Templeton did not know Souther was a spy, she should have known.

27

And when my quantity of years
has finished its dance,
a million bloodstains will lie spread
on the path to my father's house.

—VLADIMIR MAYAKOVSKY, "A Cloud
in Trousers"

THE FIRST NEWSPAPER STORY about Souther's disappearance appeared on November 9, 1986, on the front page of the Norfolk *Virginian-Pilot*. It was quickly picked up by other papers and broadcast on television and radio.

"Disappearance of ODU [Old Dominion University] grad leads to probe: Federal agents suspect spying by ex-navy man," the headline said.

Written by Steve Stone, the article said Souther had failed to return from Rome, and federal investigators feared they had another spy case on their hands. Stone's reporting was the best done on the Souther case. Yet like most of the stories to follow, the article was skimpy on details—understandable in view of the shroud of secrecy about the case. By then, it was clear to the FBI and the Justice Department that Souther was a spy and probably had defected.

The article quoted teachers and friends as saying they could not believe he was a spy.

"I have never known any spies," said Frances Hassencahl, his speech communication teacher at Old Dominion. "[B]ut it just seems to me there was no motivation. If he was doing it for money, he didn't have any. They must have been paying him very poorly."

Hassencahl added, "He wasn't against the U.S. government. He wasn't 'rah-rah' the Soviet Union. He wasn't antinavy."

Dr. Mihalap, one of his two Russian teachers, said, "They [the FBI] asked me if I knew anything negative about him. I told them absolutely not. The suspicion that he may have been a spy? It's unbelievable."[201]

In a story by United Press International that appeared in *The Washington Post*, Hassencahl was quoted as saying that Souther's fiancée, Ann McCay, believed the investigation started when Souther's former wife alleged out of spite that he was a spy. His family believed he was the victim of foul play, she said.

"My impression is that his family feels the government hasn't done enough to try and find out what happened," Hassencahl said.[202]

In the fall of 1987 a grand jury based in Norfolk began hearing evidence in the case. By then, Ann McCay was sure he was dead. She had long since canceled their condominium contract and tearfully given up on their wedding plans. Because it brought back so many memories, she also gave away their dog, Vladimir.[203]

One by one, Souther's friends and family members testified about his spy activities, finances, or political beliefs. The experience was nerve-racking. Before her appearance, Klein chain-smoked furiously. Robert J. Seidel, the assistant U.S. attorney in charge of the case, tried to be friendly. Since they both lived in Chesapeake, not far from Norfolk, he chatted about the area. Then he asked if there was anything she had forgotten to tell the FBI. She said there wasn't.

A man who appeared to be a security officer came up to her when she was sitting outside the grand jury room and engaged her in conversation just before she was to testify.

"They'll take you in a few minutes," he said.

Meanwhile, he was being aggressively friendly.

"You're not afraid, are you?" the man asked.

"No," she said.

"That's good. As long as you tell them everything, they can't do anything to hurt you," he said.

Klein decided he was a plant.[204]

When it was her turn, Seidel asked her if she wondered where Souther got his money.

"It wasn't any of my business," she said.

"Just answer the questions," Seidel said.

He asked if Souther took Cindy to Italy.

"I recall he did," she said.

Seidel asked if Souther flashed wads of cash around. Did she know where he got his money? Did he say anything anti-American? Did he seem to be a loyal American? Did he take many trips abroad? Why did he study Russian? Did she see him in Russia?

In ten minutes it was over, and the next witness was called.

Cindy was asked about the money Souther brought back from Italy. Half the time, she didn't know what Seidel was talking about.[205]

Before testifying, she had been seated in another room with Tim Souther, Souther's mother, and Souther's fiancée. She asked Tim what he knew.

"Didn't you see anything strange, too?" she asked him.

"No," he said.

"You mean I'm the only one?" she thought to herself. "Maybe they'll think I *am* involved."

Tim Souther did not like Seidel's manner and decided to tell as little as he knew.

"He was sarcastic and hard-nosed," he said. "I wasn't on trial. I kept saying all I do is build molds [for a living]. I don't know anything. Then he got really mad. He yelled at me."[206]

Meanwhile, the FBI established that despite their physical proximity, Souther was not involved with Walker, who mysteriously referred in a letter to his KGB handlers to another possible member of his ring. Designated only as "F," the suspect was located by the FBI and interrogated. The FBI concluded that Walker had hoped to recruit him but had not been able to do so. In a letter to the author, Walker said he knew nothing about Souther.[207]

As the investigation continued, the NIS finally visited Di Palma in Italy and asked her for the basis of her original allegation. She told the agents about Souther's statement that he had begun working for the Soviets through the embassy in Rome, and she described the dozens of types of tradecraft that she had seen Souther engage in.

Then the FBI interviewed her in Italy. By then the FBI's Norfolk office knew that the NIS had failed to investigate her original allegation. It was clear to the FBI that the NIS had not provided all the facts to the Bureau, and there was a feeling within the Bureau that the NIS hoped the entire matter would go away.

"The big problem as we saw it when it first came to us was they [the NIS] had screwed it up, and they knew it, and they basically said to us, 'Bail us out,' " a former FBI agent said.

A theory developed within the FBI that the NIS might not

have pursued the allegation four years earlier out of embarrassment that Di Palma was allegedly going out with an NIS agent while married to Souther. In fact, that was not the case. The idea that Di Palma had been going with an NIS agent apparently arose because she had had an affair with a navy enlisted man. When the FBI eventually interviewed her, the agents asked her if she had gone out with an NIS agent, and she said she had not. From the FBI's standpoint, that was the end of the matter.[208]

Since the NIS had originally ignored her tip, Di Palma was reluctant to cooperate with either the NIS or the FBI.

"I told the FBI, 'You didn't believe me before. Why should I do something now?' " Di Palma said. "They said, 'You have to understand, many wives say this.' "[209]

Later, when the FBI asked her to fly to Norfolk to appear before the grand jury investigating the Souther case, she stalled. Even though the FBI offered to pay her way, in view of the arrogant way the NIS had treated her, she was in no hurry to help.

By the middle of 1988, the NIS had interviewed 164 present or former employees of FICEURLANT. While no one had seen Souther remove a document, it was clear that he had had almost unlimited access to the top-secret facility. Because no record was kept of the comings and goings of employees cleared for the facility, he could have shown up there at almost any time.

"When a guy goes there on a weekend, he has the run of the building," said a retired naval intelligence official whose command included FICEURLANT.

Moreover, one employee reported having seen him at the facility during the week, when he was not supposed to be on duty.

As the navy began to examine what steps should be taken to prevent such cases in the future, a troubling question arose in the minds of some in the intelligence community charged with apprehending spies: why is it that the navy, over the years, has accounted for a disproportionate share of military spies?

Of the thirty-three military men prosecuted for espionage or unauthorized possession of classified material since 1975, no fewer than twenty-five—more than three-quarters—have been employed in the navy or marine corps, which is part of the navy. Only four each have been in the army and air force, respectively.[210] This is despite the fact that the navy, including the marine corps, has roughly the same number of active-duty military personnel as the army—789,920, compared with 771,847 for the army. The air force has 576,446 active-duty personnel.[211]

The disproportionate number of espionage cases in the navy might suggest that the navy is better at detecting espionage than the army or air force. But that is not the case. Experts in the field say that if anything, the Naval Investigative Service, which has jurisdiction for crimes committed by navy personnel, is not as good as the other military investigative services at finding and investigating espionage.[212]

Another possible explanation is that the KGB may be more interested in navy secrets, or that navy recruits have more access to secrets than recruits in the other services. Yet while the navy and air force may have more technical secrets, the army has a wide range of tactical and communications secrets. The fact that the other military services each have their share of spy cases means the KGB is interested in getting secrets wherever it can.

While no one can say for certain why the navy has more than its share of spies, those who are familiar with the problem say the navy institutionally takes security less seriously than the other services. One NIS official said the navy gives security a lower priority than other assignments.

"Security is always a secondary assignment [in the navy]," he said. "There is no such thing as someone who is trained and bred and promoted to be in security. There is no career for security work in the navy, whereas in the other services, there is. In the navy it's an insignificant little job that's given to someone who has failed in another job, and they're looking for somewhere to put him."[213]

"Security is not as good in the navy as in the other services or intelligence components," a senior intelligence official said. "The navy historically has been sloppy. All of the navy cases are good examples. They cover their asses politically. It's never been recognized as a problem from the top."[214]

Since the Walker case, the navy has expanded the number of polygraph tests given to personnel with sensitive compartmented information clearances, such as Souther had. In addition, decisions on giving clearances have been consolidated. Previously, each commander granted clearances to his own people.

"There's been a long hard fight to get approval to polygraph many of our people on a fairly regular basis," says a former naval intelligence official. "We're winning that battle now, but the greatest limitation is there are only so many polygraphers."

In a statement responding to the question of why it has a disproportionate number of espionage cases, the navy said, "There is no way to compare in quantifiable terms each service's commitment to security. The navy sees proper security measures as absolutely vital to meet its responsibilities in the defense of the U.S. The responsibility for compliance with these measures rests with each individual member of the navy family, up and down the chain of command. The navy goes to great lengths to ensure that this compliance is forthcoming. Constant command attention and continuing security education have raised the overall awareness of this responsibility."[215]*

Despite the improvement, background checks are still done haphazardly. The budget for the Defense Investigative Service, which does the investigations, was cut by $8 million in 1988, requiring a thirteen percent reduction in personnel. Yet as of that year, the Pentagon had a backlog of 101,000 people who were still due to be reinvestigated.[216]

The biggest problem remains attitude—a blasé approach that suggests that spying, like prostitution, will always occur, and there is not a lot that can be done about it.

"If a guy wants to take a diskette out in his jockstrap or a gal in her blouse, you can't stop that," a former naval intelligence official said. "As I tell people, part of it is awareness. The pros you're not going to catch. The people you catch are conscientious and are trying to take a shortcut and have a deadline to meet."

While it is true that spying will always be with us, a less-than-vigilant attitude often encourages spying. As investigators delved into some of the recent spy cases, they found that shocking security breaches had contributed to the crimes. For example, when prosecutors tried to track down all the copies of the KH-11 technical manual given by William Kampiles to the Soviets, they were amazed to find that thirteen copies of the spy satellite manual could not be located. Contrary to regulations, the navy did not reinvestigate John Walker during the twenty years he held a top-secret security clearance. The CIA misread the results of a polygraph exam of Karl Koecher, the Czech intelligence service officer who became a mole in the agency. And the CIA hired Edward Lee Howard despite his history of drug use, then trained him for Moscow. When more

*The navy's full statement appears in an appendix to this book, beginning on page 260.

signs of drug use were detected, the CIA fired him without permitting him to find another job first. He found one anyway—working for the KGB in Moscow.[217]

Despite lessons learned from such cases, many of the conditions that led to them in the first place continue. The reason Pollard was able to spy so effectively for the Israelis is that he had access, through a computer terminal, to classified information on any area of the world. Even though he was assigned to terrorist threats to North America, he was able to obtain voluminous material about the Middle East that had nothing to do with terrorism.

It would be a simple matter to reprogram the navy's computers to allow access only to geographical areas for which an employee has the codes. Similar limits are used by private industry all the time, if only to lower costs of using massive data retrieval systems. Yet to this day the navy insists on allowing unlimited geographic access to people in positions similar to Pollard's.

Other problems are more subtle. Clearly, the solution to spying is not to lock up at night everyone with a security clearance. But by suggesting that there is a conflict between good security and using intelligence effectively, some in the navy unintentionally convey the impression that security is not very important. The fact is you can have both—good security and useful intelligence. In the end, it's the amount of attention paid to security that counts.

"We had security briefings, including ones set up on things going on around the Soviet embassy," a retired naval intelligence official said. "But the commands are looking at ten thousand different things—safe driving, buy savings bonds. The ones that get the most attention have the squeaky wheels."[218]

28

Listen, mister god!
Isn't it tedious
to dip your puffy eyes
every day into a jelly of cloud?
Let us—why not—
start a merry-go-round
on the tree of what is good and evil!

—VLADIMIR MAYAKOVSKY, "A Cloud
in Trousers"

ON JULY 17, 1988, the Soviet newspaper *Izvestia* announced that Souther had been granted political asylum because he was being "unfoundedly persecuted" in the United States.

Until then, the FBI—while strongly suspecting it—was not sure that he was in Moscow. His mother, who had not heard from him for two years, still wondered if Di Palma's family had killed him. His friends from the Russian Club, not knowing any of the details of his spy activities, still thought he might have been in an accident.

The *Izvestia* article said Souther had appealed to the presidium of the Supreme Soviet for refuge in order to "hide from U.S. Special Services, which were pursuing him groundlessly."[219]

Two days later, on July 19, 1988, Souther appeared on the Soviet evening television show "Camera Looks at the World."

Suddenly, he was a celebrity and, by all appearances, enjoying the new role.

"Hi. My name is Glenn Souther. I am an American citizen," he said. Thus did Souther confirm on Soviet television that he had indeed defected.

Although he was fluent in Russian, he spoke in English, which faded into an overdubbed Russian translation.[220] For an hour, the prime-time show focused on Souther, his reactions to Soviet life, and his reasons for defecting. As the camera showed him in a television studio, Souther, attired in a gray suit, sweater, white shirt, and a red tie, spoke matter-of-factly:

> For several years, I have served in the U.S. Navy. In recent years, I have worked in the U.S. Navy Intelligence Center in the European-Atlantic zone. At the same time, I studied at the Old Dominion University in Norfolk, Virginia. There I studied Russian language and literature.
>
> Last year, I found myself having to make a decision which changed my life. I had to leave my country, family, relatives, and friends. My only fault was that I regarded my interests and convictions as my rights. The FBI thought otherwise. They started following me, deprived me of my future, and restricted my freedom.
>
> Finding myself in this situation, I approached the U.S.S.R. Presidium of the Supreme Soviet with a request to grant me political asylum. Fortunately, this request was granted.
>
> Recently, Soviet and U.S. leaders signed an exceptionally important document—the INF treaty. I am convinced that this is precisely the right path along which the Soviet, American, and other countries of the world must follow. But based on my own bitter experience, I also discovered that the American people's aspiration to live in peace is not always reflected in Washington's policies. The U.S. society lives under complex and cruel laws. Availing myself of the opportunity offered to me by Soviet television, I would like to share these thoughts with you.

The program cut to general shots of American scenes, then showed Souther walking with Dmitry Biryukov, the program's host, in the snow-covered Piskaryovskoye Memorial Cemetery outside Leningrad. As Souther stood in front of a memorial to Soviet soldiers killed during World War II, the program summarized Souther's background—born in 1957 in Hammond, Indiana, worked at the U.S. Navy base in Norfolk processing aerospace intelligence materials. The words he spoke scrolled across the screen.

The camera cut to an aerial shot of an unidentified aircraft carrier, then to a studio scene. Souther sat sideways behind a desk, a plant and venetian blinds behind him. An interviewer sat at one edge of the desk.

"As I understand it," the interviewer said, "recently you worked for an organization which is called . . ."

"U.S. Navy Satellite Intelligence Center for Europe and the Atlantic," Souther interjected. "I remember an interesting case. They were looking over the Soviet Union and photographed a peasant driving a tractor which had the words 'Happy New Year' written on it."

"So, in a certain sense, you are prepared for coming here since this is how you first got to know our country," the interviewer said.

The screen showed Souther's identification card from FICEURLANT as Souther began telling about his experiences on the U.S.S. *Nimitz*.

"It was there that I first felt some confusion regarding U.S. policies," he said, motioning with his hands. "We were told that the *Nimitz* carried nuclear weapons, even though politicians denied this. Not all, but some did."

The screen cut to file film of the *Nimitz* as Souther said other ships also carry nuclear weapons.

"The *Nimitz* was loaded to its decks with nuclear weapons.

This, in fact, caused me first to have doubts, even though at this time I was still very young and naïve," he said.

Shots of missiles deployed on the U.S.S. *Yorktown* appeared on the screen as Souther noted that the nuclear weapons were unloaded when the *Nimitz* returned home. He said not only carriers deploy the weapons.

"These weapons were also carried on slow auxiliary ships which were entrusted with providing technical support," he said.

Souther said the United States has agreements with various countries about what kinds of nuclear weapons are allowed in those countries.

"One way or the other, U.S. ships visiting foreign ports carry nuclear arms on board," he said.

"All this is fraught with enormous danger," the interviewer said.

"Naturally," Souther said, "the principle of the U.S. Navy is such that a ship's commander in certain circumstances is empowered to make a decision on the use of nuclear arms."

"Can this be done even at this level?" the interviewer asked incredulously.

"Yes," Souther said. "If he considers himself capable of using nuclear arms, he will use it, even if the permission to use it was received much earlier. Sure, if he has the permission in his pocket, he has the right to make the decision for himself. The situation demands this, and this means he has the permission. The U.S. nuclear policy proceeds from the notion that a couple of nuclear warheads are capable of ending a conflict. All combat strategic instructions for the duration of navy maneuvers in which I happened to take part say 'Aggravation of a combat situation entails a conflict involving the use of nuclear arms.' So the U.S. strategic directive itself directly involves the use of nuclear arms. Therefore, if a commander finds himself involved in an actual conflict, he, after stages one and two of combat readiness, may give the order to use nuclear arms."

As he spoke, an aircraft carrier, sections of a naval ship, and stages of a missile launch appeared on the screen. American military music played in the background.

"You know," he said, "more than anything, I am concerned with the possibility of the emergence of a mad commander of a large ship. He would be able to press that fatal button. He would press it and start the missiles."

Then Souther went on to talk about his feelings about the U.S. military—feelings very similar to those he had expressed to Cindy and others. He seemed very comfortable talking to the English-speaking host, as if they were old friends.

"While I was a U.S. serviceman in Europe, I sailed on ships in the Mediterranean," he said. "I should say that sometimes it was very difficult to be an American, especially a military one. My many years of service in the U.S. Navy convinced me that Americans themselves caused this kind of attitude. Americans, by the way, spend enormous sums in countries where their bases are located, paid to lease the land, and for other purposes. The United States considers these countries its satellites.

"My duties in naval intelligence made some interesting details available to me," he told the interviewer somewhat cockily. "For example, according to one of the NATO strategic concepts, in case of a war between the U.S. and the U.S.S.R., it was proposed to lock the Soviet navy in the Black Sea," Souther said, gesticulating animatedly. "In such a case, each NATO country would be given its own task. Greece, for example, would have to block the Soviet navy by way of mining the waters between islands. Once I happened to be at a briefing attended by U.S. senators and congressmen who inspected the U.S. Sixth Fleet in the framework of NATO. The NATO commander took the floor and argued that the U.S. was not sure whether Greece was capable of carrying out this task. It had neither mine-sweepers nor the relevant equipment. In general, it was not a very reliable NATO member, and therefore it was doubtful if it was capable of carrying out this task. Then the discussion turned to the feasibility of the U.S. joining the operation or giving the task of mining the passages to Turkey. It was carefully considered which country was more valuable to NATO. The preference was given to Turkey, not Greece."

"Did your critical attitude toward the U.S. policy play a part, or did it not, when the FBI later started following you?" the interviewer asked.

"Of course it was so," Souther said. "Many years ago, after the Camp David agreements were concluded, I served with the U.S. Sixth Fleet. We took part, with our allies, in joint visits. We first visited Egyptian and later Israeli ports. In Egypt, one of our tasks was to take photos of port military facilities and installations. But this was illegal activity," he said self-righteously. "At that time, Egypt was considered to be almost a U.S. ally. Then we sailed to Israeli shores, and again photographed the military facilities there. One of my subordinates at the time said, 'Glenn, I have nothing against spying on Egypt or one of our declared enemies, but I cannot spy on an ally.' It was incredible, and so were many other things."

At this point, he spoke as if he were informing a business colleague of a competitor's operations.

Souther cited the fact that some documents in U.S. command centers in Europe are marked "U.S. Consumers Only," meaning that they are not to be seen by NATO allies. He also said the United States is prepared to use U.S. nuclear arms in Europe without consulting NATO allies.

Next, the program showed shots of Souther visiting the Estonian Republican Committee for the Defense of Peace in Tallinn, the Estonian capital. In Russian, Souther talked with an

----

official of the committee and an official of the U.S.S.R. Peace Fund.

Souther picked up a child's doll that was sitting on a shelf in the office. Called Carlsson-on-the-Roof, it flies, among other things. One of the officials said it was one of many toys sent by the Soviet Union to Nicaraguan children. With the other official, an elderly man with a long white beard, Souther discussed the fact that the United States and the U.S.S.R. had been allies in World War II.

"We fought together. You were an ally! But what happened? Why is the U.S. so much against you? Why do they try . . . ," Souther asked.

As shots of Winston Churchill and Franklin D. Roosevelt appeared on the screen, the official said the U.S. attitude changed after Winston Churchill called on the Western world to unite against the Soviet Union.

"There are many Americans who think that the Soviet Union is a fascist state," Souther said, leaning forward on a red couch. "It's strange but true."

The elderly official asked Souther why he came to the Soviet Union.

"Why did I come?" Souther asked rhetorically. "I simply decided whether to live here, or not to live. I bought a ticket and came here."

"What about your family?" the official asked, perplexed.

"My family is still in America, and they do not know anything about this."

"They don't know anything at all?"

"Not about where I am," Souther said. "But they will find out."

"You are a desperate person," the official said, laughing. He puffed on a cigarette.

"Yes. There are certainly many difficulties. It is both good and bad here. Without my mother, without the family. It is difficult."

"Does your mother live alone?" the official asked.

"Yes," he said. "It will be interesting to see what she says when she sees this broadcast. This will be the most difficult thing. What will she think of me?"

"Have you written to her?"

"Not yet."

"She knows nothing of your being in the Soviet Union?"

"No. Not at all," Souther said.

He looked uncomfortable. Then he changed the subject. "I want to say that I like your beard a great deal," he said.

The screen next showed Souther clad in a white-and-blue sport jacket walking the streets of Moscow, shopping, and speaking with male and female friends. Then the video showed shots taken from American television shows portraying anti-Communist themes, including anti-Communist cartoons, young American students expressing fear of the Soviet Union, and vicious-looking Russians in the film *Rocky IV*.

Back in the studio, the interviewer said that in the early sixties and mid–1970s, it was not considered safe for American students to study Soviet life and Russian culture, unless it was to prepare for a career in the CIA, State Department, or journalism. The press and cinema fostered this attitude, he said.

As he talked, Souther played nervously with his hands, touching his fingertips as if counting them over and over again.

"This is undoubtedly the case," Souther said, scratching his cheek. "We can see this in many films. One can see this in the material shown by American and Soviet television. We have just seen some of it. These are the widely known *Rambo* and *Rocky*. I feel that these films are in no way indicative of the feelings of an average American or his true feelings for the Soviet Union. I think not all Americans think this way."

197

Referring to his previous visits to Leningrad and Tallinn, he said people he spoke with in those cities mentioned the period when the United States and the U.S.S.R. were allies.

"Admittedly, many Americans have forgotten this," he said. "Furthermore, there are cultural differences. For Americans, World War II is history. They now speak of the next war and think this time it will be the Soviet Union that will oppose them. As far as the Soviet people are concerned, they have no need for a war. I have yet to meet a single person in the Soviet Union—and I have met lots of them—who would like to go to war with the United States. People here are afraid of the idea of war."

The screen cut to Souther, wearing a traditional Russian fur hat, walking in Piskaryovskoye Memorial Cemetery in Leningrad. An official of the cemetery accompanied him. Solemn Russian music played in the background. The official told Souther that in one month alone in 1942 some 120,000 people were buried there.

The screen cut to U.S. planes catapulted from an aircraft carrier, fading into clips from the film *Top Gun*, then to shots of devastation and protests following the 1986 U.S. air raid on Libya—a raid the interviewer said Souther was involved in.

"We were then engaged in development of the plan for bombing Libyan targets," Souther said. "Approximately three days before the bombing, I was in one of the buildings of the intelligence center engaged in duplicating satellite photographs. One of the workers of the center came to me and said, 'Look, you won't believe this, but they will have to bomb these targets.' The French embassy was among the targets I was shown."

"While planning the strike against Tripoli, Americans intentionally ignored the fact that the French embassy was located in the killing zone," the interviewer said. "This was done because the French government refused the U.S. bombers the right of passage over French territory on their way to Libya."

"I think that the most immoral thing [done by the U.S.] was regarding the sad event of the Chernobyl accident," Souther said. "Well, a misfortune happened. Newspapers at once brought us reports on losses, numbers of deaths. The reports emphasized, 'Look! Look how many people died because of this—many thousands.' I was on duty immediately after the accident. I personally saw the photos taken by satellites and the summary of what happened, according to which the number of dead numbered nineteen or twenty. Newspapers and government documents reported thousands dead."

There was a cut to film clips of television coverage of the Chernobyl accident, as well as to U.S. newspaper clips on the accident. Then the screen showed an unidentified, ungainly satellite drifting in space and a demonstration of the tremendous resolution that photos taken by satellite can achieve, down to a license-plate number.

"If it's not covered, they can see it," Souther said. "The U.S. has satellites of different kinds on various orbits. Photographic information is transmitted by means of telemetry, on an order from earth, during a flight over a certain point. A laser of the satellite sends a photograph and an image is placed onto film. After development, a very detailed positive image is obtained. Then you can see diversified details of the photo. This is how one could have had a good idea of what happened at Chernobyl, from satellite photographs. The picture was very clear, and it provided a comprehensive assessment of the event."

"The targets chosen for photography by satellites are mainly military ones," the interviewer said. "The military is, apparently, primarily interested in military targets."

"Chernobyl was not a military target," Souther pointed out.

"Apparently, some strategic targets are also photographed," the interviewer said.

"Sometimes they are, sometimes they aren't," Souther said. "Collection of intelligence information for strategic tasks does not stop, even for propaganda reasons."

Next the screen showed Souther walking with Biryukov in Leningrad, past the famous Hermitage Museum, then going to the cruiser *Avrora*, which has been turned into a museum.

"This is a beautiful city with wonderful people," Souther said. "Those few I have associated with are real patriots of their city."

As he walked onto the bridge, he chatted with the director of the museum. Souther looked cold and tired.

"I like cities at night," Souther said, as shots of the lights of Moscow and Leningrad appeared. "When I served as a sailor, we used to enter various ports. During the day, I usually stayed on board. But at night I would take my camera and photograph whatever port we happened to be in. Now that I am living in Moscow, I like to walk in the evening and at night. Perhaps it is not quite as exciting, but it is very romantic."

The camera cut to Souther watching a television report describing the case of an American child who entered an imaginary name in an ice cream parlor contest and years later received at his address a draft notice addressed to the imaginary person. As pictures appeared of American children innocently eating ice cream at birthday parties, the announcer stated that this is the sort of lifelong surveillance Americans are subjected to.

"Yes, surveillance is a part of American life," Souther said, "and the latest technology is used."

"High-quality technology?" the interviewer asked.

"Yes, it is very easy in the U.S.," Souther said, as pictures of hundreds of rows of stored computer tapes appeared. "As you know, I had some experience with the FBI. They showed an interest in me when they found it important to know why I wanted to learn Russian. Obviously, later they began following me."

"Then it all started because of political considerations?" the interviewer asked.

"I think that in my case, the surveillance was instituted for political reasons," Souther said.

"If that is the case, my next question is as follows: I would imagine that you had serious reasons to come to the Soviet Union?"

"Uh-huh," Souther said, smiling grimly. "I have already said that I was studying Russian and that I had planned to enter the U.S. Navy," he said. "Then one fine day the FBI invited me to come in for a chat. They started asking me how things were. I told them all was well. They asked me about a college friend of mine. Then they began asking strange questions: Do you like the Soviet culture? Do you like studying about the Soviet Union? I answered in the affirmative. I told them that I was very fond of Mayakovsky. But slowly they worked their way to the main question: What brought on this interest? It is good to study the Russian language and culture to help the U.S. gain an advantage over the Soviet Union, or to gather intelligence information. However, I thought if one is sympathetic to the Soviet Union, this kind of thinking, this train of thought, can only be considered a negative factor. This depressed me."

Souther said he often visited the Victor P. Kamkin Bookstore in Rockville, Maryland, where he bought Russian-language books. After such a visit, he said, he noticed he was being watched.

"I cannot remember exactly how long it went on. I had applied for a commission in the navy, and suddenly all the progress and paperwork toward the commission was stopped," he said. "Of course, they gave no reason for stopping everything. I phoned my mother and told her that I was called in by the FBI for a talk. She decided that this is why everything concerning the commission was stopped. It is curious that when I was called to the FBI, the person speaking to me noted that they had intended to have a talk with me a year ago. However, I was constantly traveling. I lived in a summer camp, and I even rented out my apartment during the summer. Therefore, in fact, they watched me for over a year. How did they do this? I have no idea. Perhaps they did it like they did in the movies. Physically, however, they followed me like a shadow for a month and a half. They visited my friends, places I have been to, where I used to go.

"Finally, I made a decision: I bought an airline ticket and left the country. I have reason to believe that I have been very lucky. I think I was very lucky. I was being followed and I was really very lucky to have been able to get away from there." He added, "I think the FBI agents in Washington wasted a lot of time on me."

"So you chose the Soviet Union," the interviewer said. "Speaking to you, one comes to the conclusion that things have been going well for you."

"Okay," Souther said, smiling. "I have a good apartment."

"Are you able to make a living here?" the interviewer asked.

"Yes, certainly."

"I know that Americans find it important to have a car," the interviewer said.

"Yes, I do have a car," Souther said. "But I don't drive it often. Things for the most part are fine here. I am getting used to things. I have more than enough work. I have yet to find my niche in life. I feel that I am not at my most productive. I have yet to find the right pulse," he said, confidently. "It takes time to get used to another set of traditions. People are kind to me. They are very patient. Such patience is not often encountered."

"It seems that you will have to perfect your knowledge of Russian?" the interviewer said.

"Yes, certainly."

"Have you been reading Mayakovsky in Russian?" the interviewer asked.

"Yes, I am studying so that I can translate Mayakovsky into English. He is my favorite poet."

Shots of Mayakovsky exhorting a crowd appeared, then a statue of the poet in Moscow's Mayakovsky Square, a center of the city's cultural life.

"You know, his life was very interesting," Biryukov said. "His life, his biography."

"You know what I like best in Mayakovsky?" Souther asked. "It's the fact that his poetry is impossible to understand without knowing the story of his life. His poetry and his fate are closely intertwined. Mayakovsky is one of these people, one of those poets who, when he writes, bares his soul. He says, 'This is me. I have my weaknesses. Sometimes I act up, but this is what I am.'

"My favorite Mayakovsky poem is called 'A Cloud in Trousers,' " he said. "It has a line that says, 'Mother, I cannot sing in church while my house is burning.' I think that this explains the essence of Mayakovsky. He knew that he was a harsh man, a man with unrefined tastes. However, at the same time, he is a man who can be wounded and who was tormented by personal problems."

Referring to the city where Mayakovsky spent much of his life, the interviewer asked, "Now that you have visited Leningrad, has Mayakovsky become closer to you? He did write about Dvorets Square [the location of the czar's residence and the Hermitage Museum] and the October Revolution. Are you planning to travel further around our country?"

"I hope so," Souther said. "I have already visited the Baltic States, and Georgia, and of course the two of us have visited Leningrad. I hope to visit other places."

"Have you come across any bears on our streets?" the interviewer asked, referring to the Western symbol of Soviet oppression and surveillance.

"Bears?" Souther asked, looking confused for the first time. Then the meaning of the joke dawned on him. "No, no," he said, laughing.

Souther had gladly accepted his assigned role. The Soviets were picturing him as an American who had seen the light—exposed the warmongers for what they were, while advancing the cause of peace.

29

I thought you a great big god almighty,
but you're a dunce, a minute little
godlet.
Watch me stoop
and reach for a shoemaker's knife
in my boot.

—VLADIMIR MAYAKOVSKY, "A Cloud
in Trousers"

SOUTHER'S MOTHER had given him up for lost when a relative from the Washington area called to say an article in *The Washington Post* that day reported he had defected.[221] Written by Charles R. Babcock, the eighteen-inch story was the second lead on the front page of the July 18, 1988 editions.

"A missing former navy enlisted man, who had special intelligence clearances and is the subject of an FBI espionage investigation, has shown up in Moscow and been granted political asylum," the story said.[222]

The story went on to say that the Soviet newspaper *Izvestia* had announced that "Glen Michael Souter" asked for asylum because "he had to hide from the U.S. Special Services, which were pursuing him groundlessly." The newspaper identified him only as a U.S. citizen and didn't say how long he had been in the Soviet Union.

"A spokesman for the U.S. embassy said he was unaware of

the case. However, a spokesman for the FBI in Washington said that the man granted asylum is Glenn Michael Souther, a navy veteran in his early thirties, who disappeared in May 1986 shortly after graduating as a Russian major from Old Dominion University in Norfolk," the *Post* said.

The story quoted one source as saying that FBI and navy officials were concerned about Souther's disappearance "because he had special security clearances, including access to spy satellite photo data, while on duty with the Sixth Fleet in Italy in the early 1980s."

"He could give away information that could be valuable," one source said.

The article compared the case with that of Edward Lee Howard, the CIA officer who escaped to Moscow while FBI agents had him under surveillance. The difference was that the U.S. government could have had a potentially stronger case against Souther than it had against Howard if the NIS had interviewed Di Palma four years earlier.

When Wiergacz heard about the story, she called her other son, who already knew. Tim Souther had been watching the evening news while talking with a friend on the phone. When pictures of his brother flashed on the screen, Tim stopped talking and just watched, his mouth open.

During the past two years, Wiergacz had thought about her lost son every day and cried often. Yet she tried to be strong. After a while, she found it was easier not to talk about him at all than to bring up old memories and fears.

"If I brought it up, she'd get all upset," Tim Souther said.

Now Wiergacz told Tim that she was happy and sad at the same time—happy that Glenn was alive and that she knew what had happened to him, but sad that he had defected and that she might never see him again.[223]

Two days later, when the Associated Press ran a story about Souther's charge that the United States intentionally bombed the French embassy in Libya, Pentagon spokesman Dan Howard called the allegation "absolute garbage."

"It was a targeting problem, an accident," the spokesman told reporters. "It certainly was not done intentionally."[224]

Indeed, Souther's rambling monologue on Soviet TV had been a patchwork of truths, untruths, and facts taken out of context. While it was true that the FBI asked him why he was taking Russian and what he thought of another student, it was not true that the Bureau had followed him for a year. The reason the FBI asked about the other Russian student was that Souther himself, to make himself look better, had falsely reported that Sapozhnikov had tried to recruit him to work for the Soviet Union. The FBI asked Souther why he was taking Russian because he had a top-secret security clearance. Therefore, any interest he showed in the Soviet Union beyond what was required by his work was of legitimate concern to the government.

It is possible that Souther thought he was being followed, since the FBI agents had mentioned that they had been trying to find him for a year. Since he was paranoid under the best of circumstances, it would have been easy for him to imagine, in retrospect, that strange cars he had noticed in his neighborhood might have been FBI cars. He also may have legitimately believed that the FBI's interest in him led to his rejection by Officer Candidate School. In fact, he had already been rejected before the FBI learned anything about him from the NIS. Souther may genuinely have believed that U.S. laws are "complex and cruel," according to those who knew him. But the truth was that the FBI had not followed him—and that was the problem. If the FBI had known what was behind Di Palma's allegation, it would have put him under surveillance. Presumably, he then would not have been able to escape to the Soviet Union.

Some of Souther's other allegations were true but came as no surprise. For example, while the U.S. government does not confirm it, it is well-known that U.S. ships carry nuclear weapons, as do Soviet ships. In April 1989 the Soviets lost a submarine in the Norwegian Sea carrying what American authorities said were nuclear-tipped cruise missiles.[225] Nor is it any secret that the United States may not believe each NATO ally is as staunch and capable as the next. The fact that the United States may consider using nuclear weapons within a NATO country without consulting that country first is recognized as a possibility if the country has already been overrun by the enemy; it is therefore enemy territory. Spying on allies like Israel, while officially denied, is recognized within the intelligence community as a necessary fact of life. In the same manner, both the United States and the Soviet Union deny officially that they use spy satellites, yet the fact that they exist is as commonly known as the fact that both countries develop chemical and biological weapons. Official denials are made because governments fear that if such snooping is publicly acknowledged, the other side will be forced by pressure from its own populace to object.

As for the claim that navy commanders alone can authorize use of nuclear weapons, Souther himself pointed out that they can only launch such weapons after receiving approval through the chain of command. Moreover, the weapons cannot be launched without the consent of two duty officers on board ship.

Perhaps the most intriguing of the allegations was that the U.S. Selective Service System uses entries in ice cream parlor birthday drawings as a way of hounding kids to register for the draft. At first blush, the allegation seems to be something an imaginative KGB officer made up in his head. Yet it was true.

Since 1980 young men have had to register for the draft within thirty days of their eighteenth birthday. Failing to register can be punished by a fine of up to $10,000 or up to five years in jail, or both. To enforce the law, the Selective Service obtains lists of young men and their birth dates from motor vehicle records, high school graduation lists, Social Security records, and tax filings with the Internal Revenue Service. It then reminds those who have not registered that they must register. Young men who have not done so after several reminders may be prosecuted by the Justice Department.

In 1983, while compiling such lists, the Selective Service System bought from a broker a list of "birthday club" members from Farrell's Ice Cream Parlor, a national chain owned by the Marriott Corporation. To obtain a free sundae on their birthdays, kids under ten years of age filled out a form listing their names, addresses, and birthdays.

Some six years earlier, Eric Hentzel, then seven, and his brother, Greg, eleven, had tried to win extra free sundaes at their local Farrell's in Palo Alto, California, by entering fake names at their own addresses.

"We made up really phony names and put different birthdays on but our own address," Eric told *The Washington Post*. One such name was "Johnny Klomberg." Other names were Mickey Mouse and Santa Claus.[226]

Sure enough, when the imaginary Klomberg would have turned eighteen, he got a notice at the Hentzel's address reminding him to register. He hadn't even gotten a free sundae.

"If it [the coupon] came, I didn't notice it," Eric said.

Hentzel's father wrote a letter to the Palo Alto *Times Tribune*, which gave the story big play. It was soon picked up by media around the country. Farrell's, in responding, said it had never authorized the broker to sell the list to the government and withdrew the names from use. The Selective Service returned the list of names and said it would not use such lists again.[227]

Among other things, the Selective Service realized that the lists could include many phony names. Beyond that, the agency came to understand that ice cream and kids were emotional issues, even if the law does mandate compliance. Within the Selective Service, the matter is now referred to as the "ice cream fiasco." But the Soviet portrayal failed to note that the practice had stopped five years earlier.

Souther's claim that the United States had intentionally bombed the French embassy in Libya made no sense—even recognizing that the United States has engaged in foolish and outrageous ventures, such as selling arms to a belligerent country like Iran in an effort to release hostages. "We would have gained nothing from that," a navy intelligence officer with knowledge of the bombing said.

As news organizations scrambled for more details of Souther's defection, a theory arose that Souther had defected because he had been rejected for Officer Candidate School. In turn, the rejection was blamed on the fact that Souther had a police record because he had bitten a young woman at Old Dominion.

"I know he was very discouraged at being rejected by Officer Candidate School," Fahey, his adviser at Old Dominion, told the local CBS television affiliate in Norfolk. "I think that caused this."

A similar claim appeared on the front pages of the July 24, 1988, *Virginian-Pilot* and *Star-Ledger*.

The stories infuriated Cynthia Kotulak, the young woman Souther had bitten.

"I thought it was behind me, and he ends up as a Russian

spy and in Moscow," Kotulak said. "I get angry every time I think about it."[228]

Like a stone thrown in a lake, the news of Souther's defection caused ripples throughout the country. Each of Souther's friends and family members reacted differently. King Butterworth's sister called her from North Carolina. She had just seen the story on television.

"What's Glenn's last name?" she asked.

Butterworth was dumbstruck when her sister told her that Souther had defected. Having worked at NSA and decided she didn't like it, Butterworth was sensitive about the damage spies could do.

"It's very frustrating to me because I did work in the intelligence community," she said. "I remember how mad it would make me feel that Ron Pelton [the former NSA employee who spied for the Soviets] was trying to give away what I was trying to protect. And then here he turns around and does this," she said.

After seeing the videotape of his appearance on Soviet television, she said, "He looks very tired. I hadn't seen him for years and then all of a sudden this. I just wonder how long he thought about this. I wonder if it was a rational decision."[229]

After his disappearance, Danine Klein realized Souther could be dead. If he wasn't dead, he was in a lot of trouble.

"I almost wanted to know he was dead to get the grieving over with," she said. "It would have been easier to know he was dead."

On the other hand, now that he was alive, Klein realized she would probably never see him again.

"Mr. Fahey said he'd wrap the Soviets around his little finger the way he always did," she said. "He had influential, older tenured professors testifying to his moral character at the disciplinary proceedings [after the biting incident]."[230]

Klein thought Souther looked unnatural on Soviet TV. Not only had he shaved off his beard; his features did not seem mobile.

"He had a face that was always moving, and his eyes were full of expression. But Soviets do not smile as much as we do. He's obviously becoming more like them," she said. "Usually he bounced off the wall, cracking jokes and making wisecracks. He seemed like an automaton. His eyes didn't have that shine and sparkle."

Perhaps he was brainwashed, she thought. Or else he was depressed. "Maybe they gave him drugs. You never know. It might have made him more docile," she said.

"I wonder what he's doing there," she mused. "He's probably being pumped for information. Once they're done with him I have no idea what he would do. He'll probably find a girl. He's such a people person. He craved women and affection and all that goes with it. I can't see him going for long without several partners. Whether he'll change his *modus vivendi* is questionable. I can't see him changing."

Klein showed a visitor Souther's inscription in a book of Anna Akhmatova's poems he gave her:

Danine—I really felt badly when you called. I always get the feeling you are a person who is filled with so much love, and yet you've never given your fair share back. This book is not a present but something to put a smile on your face—and you know what kind of smile I like to see! Remember when you smile, that smile is supposed to reach all the way down to your heart and leave a peaceful, happy expression there. Enjoy these poems. My eyes were drawn to the book at Kampkin's. I could only think of you. Someone who will always love you, Glenn.

"Now I feel angry at Glenn for leaving us and his family and letting us worry so much," Klein said. "And keeping such a big secret from us and not being the person we thought he was. That he could go and leave us all without a word. I understand he couldn't. But it still hurts to have someone act so callously, to be abandoned by a friend. But mostly I'm just sad for him because I question his ability to find happiness there. If he does want to come back, he either won't be able to come back, or he will be in prison.

"I'm glad he survived," she said, "but if he were dead I wouldn't have nagging thoughts in my mind. I keep missing him. He was such a big part of my life. For the longest time and even now I would think, 'Glenn would love that' or 'He'd love to hear that story,' and I can't share it with him. I'm glad he's not dead. I don't wish him to be dead. But it would have been easier to deal with if he were dead."

Klein met some navy men at a bar where she was working as a bartender for the summer. The subject of spies and Souther came up, and one of them said, "I'd like to strangle him."

Without revealing that she knew him, Klein said, "Put yourself in his shoes. His dream all his life is to become a navy officer, and because of this prank he couldn't fulfill his lifelong dream and couldn't use his Russian. He couldn't find his place in life, like a Dostoevsky character."[231]

"Well," one of them said, "that's possible, but there's never any justification for betraying your country."

"I don't think he should be in prison unless he did compromise national security," she said. "I don't think he did. I can't believe he did anything to hurt this country. You'll never convince me of it."

One of them pointed out that Souther was over there, not here. Flight suggested he was guilty, he said.

"If he ever comes back, the death penalty would be too good for him," the man said.

The conversation unsettled Klein. Like other members of

the Russian Club, she was in a difficult position, torn by loyalty to a friend and loyalty to her country. Since she was in the dark about what Souther may or may not have done, she had no way of knowing that he was, in fact, not deserving of her trust.

Sometimes, Klein wondered if she should try to get in touch with him. Would he want to write back? If he wanted to, would he be allowed to write back? she wondered. If he could, would they allow him to say what he wanted to say? Would the mail be allowed through? Would the U.S. Postal Service intercept it?

"There are so many ifs. Would writing be interpreted by the FBI as proving I knew something?" she wondered.

"Better to keep to myself," she decided. "Probably they wouldn't tell me where he is. The Soviets are masters at bureaucratic methods."

30

Let me in!

—VLADIMIR MAYAKOVSKY, "A Cloud
in Trousers"

IN SEPTEMBER 1988, Shirley and Joe Wiergacz were allowed to visit Souther in Moscow. For more than a week, he showed them around the city and described his new life. By then, he had married a Soviet woman, and he had a young daughter by her.

As a rule, defectors are debriefed for as long as one or two years, then retained by the KGB as consultants in case their advice is needed on particular issues. For example, the KGB may be evaluating a new U.S. Navy project or obtaining biographical data on a new officer. Souther might then have been called in to give his opinion.

Souther presented a stiff upper lip to his mother and stepfather. He had never confided in them about his spying activities. He was not about to begin now. After the trip, Shirley Wiergacz told Tim Souther that his brother had said he was not a spy.

"She [his mother] said he said he's not a spy but is afraid. He wouldn't say anything about it," Tim Souther said.[232]

Meanwhile, Souther met with State Department representatives in Moscow and stated that he had voluntarily defected. This is a routine procedure that both superpowers participate in whenever a citizen defects.

For those he left behind, life went on. In Norfolk, Ann McCay tried to forget about her fiancé. She told friends she did not want to talk about him, and she soon found a new boyfriend. When he first disappeared, she gave his mother his books but kept his furniture, including his stereo, in case he came back. Later, Tim Souther complained to his mother that she, not McCay, should have taken his furniture.

"You're giving it all to Ann, and Ann isn't even family," he said. "Who knows where she'll be in two years?

"Ann doesn't stay in touch. We know nothing about her now," he said.[233]

Meanwhile, Tim had to deal with his mother, who got mad at him for consenting to be interviewed for this book. To Tim, it seemed his mother was being unrealistic. "What can I say that's going to change anything?" he asked rhetorically. "I don't know what he did or nothing. You don't know. I try not to torture myself."

One night over dinner in a restaurant, Joe Wiergacz mentioned Vladimir, Souther's dog who was named after Mayakovsky. Shirley became angry at her husband for revealing too much to Tim about her son's activities, according to Tim. Somehow, she was afraid that the fact that Souther had named his dog after a Russian poet might be seen as confirming his spy activities.[234]

Cindy was not surprised by Souther's defection, having believed for some time that he was a spy.

"Right now I feel absolutely nothing [about Glenn]. Talking

about Glenn is like talking about a character in a book, like Huckleberry Finn," she said.

She continued to regret not reporting him.

"If anyone had encouraged me, I would have gone to the FBI. For a year, it drove me crazy," she said.

Di Palma alternately had feelings of rage and longing for Souther.

"I don't understand why the Soviets trust him. He doesn't deserve trust," she said.

But after watching a video of Souther's appearance on Soviet television, she said, "It [watching the video] was painful. I wish he was here and that we were still married, maybe. I'll never forget him.[235]

"If I had known what he was doing, maybe I would have tried to help him get out of it," she said. "But he didn't give me a chance. I kept writing to my mother-in-law. She would say on the phone, 'I don't have time to write, but I love Angelo and will send a package to him for his birthday or for Christmas.' The last one was in 1987."[236]

Di Palma has had no contact with Souther's father. "At Christmas, I sent him Christmas cards with pictures of Angelo. He never answered," she added.

Fahey predicted Souther would return. "The man does have a keen intellect," he said. "When you peel away all the clowning, he has a good mind. I don't think it will be satisfied in the Soviet Union. I think we'll hear from him again."[237]

Mihalap found it difficult to think ill of Souther and worried about the kind of life he faced in the Soviet Union.

"I can assure you, I'm not paid by the KGB to give you a good picture of Glenn, but I would do an injustice to myself if I tried to say something that was not true," he said. "I still can't believe really that he did that," he said.

Others were less charitable.

"Glenn was only loyal to himself," Jon Berryman said. "As far as the navy goes, he wanted from the navy what he could get out of the navy, I think. That's probably the way he looks at the Soviets now. He wants from them what he can get out of them. They probably look at him the same way."[238]

"I think the majority of us were a bunch of naive college students who went along with the flow," he continued. "Even when that thing happened with the [biting incident], a lot of people were on his side even though he was in the wrong.

"I don't think I even know half of what was going on in Glenn's life. I think I was a very small part of his life. I didn't really know him that well. I think he was aware of that—that a lot of people didn't know him that well," he said.

Joyce Cleveland, his friend from Maine, figured Souther had done it, but not for financial reasons.

"I felt there had to be a moral reason, that he morally felt what our country was doing was not right," she said. "But I also was not shocked to hear he had done something, just because of his personality. He could do it; I believe he did it. I can't remember him saying anything against the U.S. But he's a user," she said.

31

You can't stop me.
I may be wrong
or right,
but I'm as calm as can be.
Look—
again they've beheaded the stars,
and the sky is bloodied with carnage!

—VLADIMIR MAYAKOVSKY, "A Cloud
   in Trousers"

ESPIONAGE is one of the most heinous crimes one can commit. To sell out one's country is to do collective damage to one's family, neighbors, friends, and homeland. Even in these days of *glasnost* and *perestroika,* the need for intelligence and protecting American military secrets remains vital. Without intelligence to find out what the other side is doing and counterintelligence to protect U.S. secrets, all the troops, missiles, planes, and ships in the world are useless. And so, even during a time of diminishing tensions, spy activity on both sides continues unabated and even increases as each tries to verify what the other side is doing.

Why would a young man like Glenn Souther begin working for the other side? A man with a conservative midwestern upbringing, who got outstanding ratings in the navy, who earned the respect of his professors in college? How could a young man with such a wide circle of impressive, bright friends, who

---

endeared himself to colleagues, who enjoyed the freedoms and material comforts of the United States, end up a spy?

Still seeking the answers to those troubling questions in June 1989, I presented the details of Souther's life and character to Roger Depue, who had retired two months earlier as the chief of the FBI's behavioral science unit. Souther was still alive at the time, having been in Russia then for three years. Back in 1984, I had interviewed Depue when I was a reporter for *The Washington Post* writing a story about the FBI's crime-profiling techniques. Now Depue is president of his own behavioral science consulting firm, Academy Group Inc., named for the FBI Academy where he once worked.

Based in Manassas, Virginia, the company is made up of former FBI agents from the FBI's behavioral science unit or experts who helped them, including Dr. Bertram S. Brown, former chief of the National Institute of Mental Health, and Lloyd P. Anderson, a former chief pilot of Eastern Airlines. The agents themselves specialized in solving homicides, unexplained deaths, and sexual crimes, and in dealing with hostage taking and terrorism. In addition to their investigative experience, each has advanced degrees in behavioral sciences. Depue himself has a B.A. in psychology, an M.A. in society and the law, and a Ph.D. in counseling and development. Before joining the FBI in 1968, Depue was the police chief of Clare, Michigan. By pooling their knowledge from different behavioral sciences, the firm's members help identify security threats to private industry.

Having been in charge of analyzing and profiling not only some of the most notorious criminals in the country but also most of the espionage suspects apprehended by the FBI, Depue was uniquely qualified to answer my questions. If Souther's case had been submitted to the behavioral science unit before the FBI interviewed Souther in 1986, Depue would have been in charge of developing a profile of him and helping to plan a strategy for obtaining his confession.

Standing more than six feet tall, with bulging, toned muscles and a tanned, handsome face, Depue at fifty-one looks more like a high school tight end from Detroit, where he was born, than a state-of-the-art Sherlock Holmes. He talks slowly, deliberately, with a trace of a lisp, almost as if he were purposely trying to come across as an average Joe. But behind the wide-set eyes and jutting jaw is a brain as sharp and incisive as any I have come across in twenty-five years as a reporter.

I met with Depue at his home in Catlett, Virginia. Off a rutted country road in cow pastures tended by Mennonites, the brick-and-cedar house has no street number. Depue offered decaffeinated coffee from a thermos, and we sat around a dark wood table in his family room. Depue had made no agreements about how much he would say. But after nearly four hours discussing the FBI's behavioral science unit and its work, Depue asked, "Why don't you tell me a little bit about this guy?"[239]

I outlined Souther's life, beginning with his birth in Hammond, Indiana; his predilection for wearing Confederate uniforms as a child; his obsessive and abusive need to masturbate alone in his room; and his resentment of his rather cold father.

As it turned out, Depue not only provided a profile of Souther and why he did what he did, but also offered tips he might have given FBI agents on obtaining his confession.

"Let me throw this concept out to you," he began. "When people are little children and they are abused physically or psychologically, whether by their parents or peers, they often have one recourse. That recourse is fantasy. What they do is get back at a person in their minds. It takes individual roots but basically it's something like 'If I were big enough, this is what I would do.' Or 'If I were powerful enough, what I would like to do is this.'

"It's believed that some kids get so involved in that method of trying to justify or rationalize or create equity out of this very unfair situation that this might be the thing that leads to social isolation, or actually enjoying being by yourself and having these thoughts," he said.

"We think to some extent that from these origins these fantasies are refined, elaborated upon, and are acted out. You might find that he did things to animals or insects. It's the old story of kicking the dog. You might pass it down to the younger child. Some of these kids enjoy taking the wings off a fly or tormenting or killing a cat. So you've got this beginning of a fantasy. Also the best criminals are frequently the oldest [in their families]. They are intelligent and they come from broken homes.

"But one thing we found," Depue continued, "was that the father is a cold figure in the life of the boy. Not much has been said about fathers in the literature. Most is about mothers. What we found in most of these criminals is the father is cold with most of these criminals and distant."

Studies by the University of California at Los Angeles have confirmed a connection between one's relationship with one's father and one's degree of patriotism.

"There's a significant relationship between early attachments to one's father and attachment to one's country," according to Seymour Feshbach, professor of psychology at UCLA.[240]

Depue said the distant relationship with his father could have accounted in part for Souther's tendency to dress in Confederate uniforms—to take the other side, in effect.

"That's really indicative of the fantasy that's going on there," he said. "That's part of his plan for dealing with an unjust world. Even way back in those early days you see the fantasy beginning. You see this as one of the outward manifestations of what's happening. That's 'If you can't join them, fight them.' It's the opposite of 'If you can't fight them, join them.' I think that's all significant and fits together very well. All of that is early fundamental construction of personality. In particular this fantasy."

It was one way a normal child tries to "come to grips with his environment," Depue said.

Spending a lot of time alone in a room and masturbating compulsively "is very typical of social isolates," Depue said.

Not that Souther came across as a loner. Quite the opposite.

"He did all right on the outside but didn't get his satisfaction on the outside. He got his satisfaction when he was alone," he said. "So you have all the groundwork laid there really perfectly in terms of a person who is now predisposed in adulthood for when the world isn't just to him, for him to take this kind of behavior and use this kind of acting out. These people begin to prefer their own company to the company of others, and they see people as ways of satisfying certain of their desires. They are to be manipulated or used to satisfy their needs. The person in isolation in his own room with his own thoughts tries to draw out of himself his own nurturing. Masturbation could very well be part of that. He doesn't get anything else from others of value. Every time he reaches out, his hands are whacked—his parents divorce, and there's the tremendous injustice of this other kid in his life [the friend who had been teased because he was overweight and died young]."

Depue said the death of the overweight friend could have symbolized for Souther what might happen to him—the person seen as an outcast that everyone picks on. In response, Souther decided, "That's not going to happen to me."

"But it seems that the sexual thing, the masturbation, would grow out of being by himself and fantasizing about what he is going to do. It's trying to get some kind of positive feeling. I wouldn't be surprised if that sexuality is tangled up with a lot of things in his life," he said.

At that point, a sort of Socratic interchange began, with Depue asking questions or making points while I answered or responded with relevant facts.

"I was going to say," I interjected, "that he was very preoccupied with his sexual life. He would joke about homosexuals, he would moon people, he wore a girlfriend's bra."

"I wouldn't be surprised if in his room he was doing a lot of experimental things with clothing," Depue said. "Maybe cross-dressing. Probably does pornography. When you have the fantasy like this, you have the fuel. You are sensitive to what will enhance it. Did he have sisters?"

"One," I told him.

"So he had access to clothes he could cross-dress with. A lot of times these kids will be window peepers, Peeping Toms. You usually don't find out about that unless you ask. Usually they are discovered by somebody. Of the serial murderers, eighty percent were Peeping Toms. Serial rapists were sixty-eight percent Peeping Toms. What that means is it's part of the developmental process. They learn a lot—how to move with stealth undetected in people's yards. Later some graduate into going into homes. You learn how to neutralize dogs. You learn a lot that is valuable later."

Turning to Souther's penchant for mooning people, Depue observed, "Frequently people with these sexual hang-ups expose themselves. Usually the exposing is done to get a reaction and create a shock rather than to get sexual gratification. People who window-peep and make obscene phone calls also frequently expose themselves. It's all part of this big fantasy. There's probably more to this masturbation, especially now that you say he exposed himself."

I noted that the mooning was not seen as hostile.

"I'd say it all fits together into this construction of a fantasy and maintaining and continuing to refine it, and adding to it," Depue said.

Depue asked if the Soviets had used women to blackmail Souther or control him.

"I don't think so," I said. "That is the mystery—how did he start? He did become an ideological spy and espoused Communism."

"As you know, being a Confederate in early life is very similar and symbolic—going to the other side," Depue said. "It really doesn't make any difference which side."

"He described the Soviets as not being as strong as we are," I said.

"That would fit, too," he said. "His relationship with his son sounds very much like his father's relationship with him. There's a lot of superficiality, but when you come down to what does he do, he doesn't act like a father. Nor did his father."

Depue noted that there aren't many ideological spies. Most spies—John A. Walker, Jr., Ronald W. Pelton, Army Warrant Officer James W. Hall III—engage in espionage for the money. Even Jonathan Jay Pollard, who claimed to be motivated by love for Israel, doubled his take-home pay with spy payments from the Israelis.

"Probably you're going to find several motivations," he said. "They're kind of twisted in there together. You have this childish thing which almost predisposes him to taking the other side whenever he is treated unjustly. So the question I have is, is he truly an ideological person or is it a psychological thing he does? There's a subtle difference. One is, 'I believe in this system.' The other is, 'You bastards, I'm going to take this side more for vengeance or retaliation.' "

"People felt he was vengeful," I said. "For example, he never forgave his stepfather for hitting him once."

Often, spies feel they have an entitlement to spy because an authority figure like an employer has done them wrong, Depue said.

"People believe they have something coming to them," he said. "When it doesn't come, they feel justified in doing something. Like stealing from their employers."

Despite Souther's obvious competence and success with his peers, Depue characterized Souther as an inadequate type of person—not truly inadequate, but someone who felt that way.

"Inadequacy has nothing to do with level of intelligence or capability," Depue said. "It has to do with how one feels about himself and also how he measures up to what he thinks he should measure up to. If you have great aspirations, and don't attain them, then you feel inadequate. You feel less than what you should be."

Those feelings of inadequacy probably account for Souther's bizarre pranks, he said.

"People who are constantly trying to get attention have low self-esteem," he said.

Depue noted that Souther was rated an outstanding sailor but didn't become an officer and was resentful of the navy.

"This is where I would look at the concept of entitlement that we talked about briefly," he said. "If you work at a place and you're supposed to be at your desk and have a half hour for lunch or dinner, and the only place to eat takes fifteen minutes to walk to, so you have to rush to get there and back, you might begin to feel the damn place owes you," Depue said.

"He complained he had a boss he didn't like when he began spying," I noted.

"So what happens is you begin to rationalize that you have something coming to you, and that you're entitled to more. This is a motivation for people stealing from their employer. 'If he's not going to give me what I'm worth, by God, I'll get it some way.' A lot of people in government service are frustrated like that. The lower level may feel they're worth more and steal."

At the time of my talk with Depue, interviewing Souther was still a possibility, and he suggested that one successful approach would be to explore with Souther his feelings of inadequacy and why he felt he was entitled to engage in spying.

"It's kind of like what the criminal justice system did in the sixties and seventies: 'You didn't have a chance. You were born into this horrible environment. The reason you did this is you didn't have a chance.' They didn't look at the ninety percent of kids who also were born into that environment and didn't get into trouble."

Because of the level of his social skills, Souther would enjoy being interviewed, Depue said.

"Sometimes some of the things these people do are very clever. He might want to brag about it," Depue said.

The fact that he told his girlfriends about his exploits would tend to indicate this, I said.

"Yes, but if you didn't handle that carefully, it would be a stupid thing to do," Depue said. "But the fact that he pulled it off would be a smart thing. You can build upon the fact that he was able to pull it off. Telling his girlfriends means he was trying to build a record and get attention," he said. "Many times criminals are caught that way."

Depue said it sounded as if he did not do a lot of homework.

"Some criminals will read a lot and try to improve their proficiency. Some burglars will converse with other criminals and try to learn more techniques and improve on the techniques. A lot of people in the spy business are like that—they really make an effort," Depue said.

In contrast to Souther, John Walker does not feel inadequate, Depue said.

"He is the flip side of this guy. He's got a very strong personality, an inflated ego rather than a deflated one. He thinks he's far better than he is. He takes a great deal of pride in doing what he does. He's on the psychopathic side," said Depue, who worked on the Walker family case.

"Walker is more like a real good criminal," he said. "This guy is kind of like a guy who is drifting along looking for a cause. This thing comes up and he attaches himself to it. It could have been other things," he said.

"He was a born-again Christian," I said.

"Have you read Eric Hoffer's *The True Believer?* A certain kind of personality is predisposed to getting involved in causes and goes from one cause to another," Depue said.

"He's a lot like [Christopher] Boyce," I said, referring to the protagonist in *The Falcon and the Snowman.* "They were both young, resented their father, thought the U.S. was terrible. Both were relatively low-level employees. They definitely spied less for money and more for revenge."

"I'd say probably more because of disenchantment along with revenge," Depue said. "Kind of like striking back at society and striking back at the institutions and the government and everything it stands for."

"He was doing that in other ways," I said. "For example, his crudity, the biting incident."

"The biting is interesting. He only did that once?" Depue asked.

"Yes, but he would nip at waitresses' heels at restaurants, acting like a dog. He just met the girl in the dorm once and bit her on the neck and gave her a hickey. He said, 'I'll never grow up,'" I noted. (I would later learn that he had done the same thing to another young woman.)

Reacting to the biting incident, Depue said, "That's strange. Did he use any drugs? Was he drinking?"

"He had had some beers," I said.

"We're talking about the use of alcohol prior to these events, which lowers the inhibitions and makes him more likely to do these things. A person under the influence frequently tells you things about what they're thinking about more deeply," he said. "It's another element of being unsettled. One thing all of us like and are frustrated about is sex. Somebody who masturbates enough to get lesions also is moving from sexual satisfaction into masochism. Now in an effort to get sexual satisfaction, he's actually hurt himself. That's kind of interesting. Then running this girl down and jumping on her is the flip side, the sadistic side. So you see both of these things. I wouldn't be surprised if he sexually abused his wives and was involved in some bizarre kinds of activities," Depue said.

I mentioned that Souther beat his wife at least once but always projected an image of concern.

"It sounds like sexually he's kind of open to trying anything. There's a guy who feels this is an area where he has unrestricted freedom. Whereas in the rest of his life he can't get away with too much. He can do this by himself and with others," Depue said.

"He could also be sympathetic and tender to people even though he didn't act that way," I said. "He left his mother in the dark and never saw his son. Yet people had the impression he was a caring person."

"You know we put these labels on people like 'psychopath,' " Depue said. "They almost never fit perfectly. I've known psychopaths who showed love. Sometimes not for people but for their pets. At night they go out and slit the throats of young women, yet if something happens to their pet, they feel terrible. So it's hard to compartmentalize. Sometimes you see these extremes. Sometimes drugs or alcohol allow you to slip out of the inhibitions. Having social skills and being warm and tender under certain circumstances is not necessarily incongruent with the rest of the picture."

Depue asked how manipulative Souther was.

"Very. That was one of his major characteristics," I said.

"Probably a lot of the warmth was being manipulative," Depue said. "Showing the warmth and sincerity. If that's the case you're moving closer to the person who is able to mask human emotions and pretend, but there's no depth. He uses it to maneuver and get what he wants. That's not unusual for a person of his background—a cold father and a person who had a divorce, and everything around him is falling apart. He's like a guy who has two or three loves in a row and each one turns bad. He decides he can't get involved in this anymore. 'I can't afford to put my trust and faith in people because it will hurt me.' It's an emotional blunting. They don't let themselves go too far. Sometimes they can have a better relationship with an animal because they're in control of them, and animals can't hurt them."

I mentioned that he immersed himself in the life and works of Mayakovsky.

"Did he read books about spies?" Depue asked.

"No," I said. "He said he would love it in Russia. But he also postured, pretending to be a loyal American."

"For a guy to take these courses and read books and learn Russian suggests a pretty strong feeling for the Russians," Depue said. "The ideology may have been stronger than I would have thought. It sounds like he was able to learn it very well."

"A Russian émigré said he understood the Russian soul," I said.

"Let's look at that from the standpoint of escapism, that the grass is always greener. Where is utopia and how do you get there? It's his fantasy for someday having everything turn out right. The whole series of women suggests something like that. It's not working so you switch to another one."

Depue said working in a secret intelligence center could figure in Souther's fantasy as well.

"I've seen that before," he said. "People enamored by access. They would boast about it, sometimes."

"He didn't," I said.

Depue said he didn't need to. He had the same kind of outlet with the Soviets.

"He was going to the people from whom he gets his kudos," he said.

"What you said about escapism might also relate to this attitude that the Russians are the underdogs," I said. "He said the U.S. controls everything, and the Soviets would never start a war."

"He's drawn to a representative of the victim, the underdog," Depue said. "I can't help but get the feeling it's retaliatory. He would play on your side if you let him. We won't let him so he plays on the other side. He wanted to go to Officer Candidate School.

"I wonder about the Soviets' ability to manipulate him," Depue continued. "Here you have a person who is very frustrated about his life-style. At what point did he go to the Soviets to spy?"

"In 1980," I said.

"What was going on in his life?"

"He was drinking a lot, seeing other women, then began abusing his wife," I said.

"So he's having extramarital things, some friction with the wife. Did he speak Italian?"

"Yes, he learned it very well. He spoke Russian well."

"Did he ever have a relationship with an American woman?" he asked.

"His girlfriends and finally a fiancée," I said.

"It sounds like wherever he is he finds somebody. Sounds like he's impulsive, which is the opposite of commitment. Whether or not he had commitments to people or ideas that showed any kind of depth or long-term interests, I don't know," he said.

"Just the opposite," I said. "He had friendships that never lasted after he moved. He said he didn't like to keep ties."

Depue could see Souther as wanting to return. In retrospect, Depue's assessment of Souther's eventual disenchantment is uncanny.

"What I'm thinking is that if you look at his life-style and short-term commitment and moving on without looking back, and not really feeling very much—he kind of gets in the car and drives away. It seems to be kind of a naïveté, a bit of distance from the real world," he said.

"Chances are if he's been there a couple of years, he knows it's not utopia. It's like those kids of the 1960s and 1970s realizing that our form of democracy isn't all that bad. It's not perfect, but it's not all that bad. What's the possibility of having him doing the ultimate, coming back? We're trying to look at it through his eyes. Maybe that would be the ultimate kick.

"There are people who are good at creating things but not maintaining them," Depue added. "They're searching for the next thing. It's possible his personality is something like that. He may be searching for something to make his life meaningful and worthwhile."

I mentioned my efforts to obtain an interview with Souther and indications he might agree to one.

"This is something he needs right now," he said. "He needs to talk to someone who understands these matters. It's very similar to the murders we do, where we have two experts who sit down on the opposite side of the table. I can see where he would want to talk to people about it. He's probably trying to understand himself, trying to sort some things out. I would say it would be very easy to get into a conversation about some of these things in order for him to examine them. He would want to come away with a little insight into his own behavior. There may be something in it for him. If he's not happy over there, he would have to be thinking about what his next move is. I could see him thinking, 'Damn, what do I do now? I'm thirty-two years old.' I don't suppose the Russians have given him a penthouse anywhere. He's probably living some normal existence, which would be subnormal compared with our life-style."

"He liked to live well, drink fine wines, get custom-made Italian clothing," I said.

"If he were a true Marxist and his ideology were heavy, he would get to the basic theory of Marxism, and I would think there is reason for disenchantment by a true ideologue, once he gets over there and sees what it's supposed to be fifty years later, and it's not. There are not only economic but societal problems.

"The more you can create that atmosphere of two experts sitting down, it will be to your benefit," Depue said. "It sounds like his childhood was unfortunate. That has a way of setting you up for a fall. I would think this guy would be really susceptible to any approach that would make him feel he was important, and his life is worthwhile. Also, he's been able to do things that no one else has done and probably many people have thought about. He could share the reality of doing something that others know about only in fantasy.

"You might want to start first with the material you know about, his childhood and what he did that in his eyes was successful," Depue continued. "Toward the end I would ask him some of those tough questions: What does he think about some of these recent events in the Soviet Union as well as China?

233

What do they mean? One almost has to conclude that it's not Marxism. If you read Marx, this is not the way it's supposed to be."

"He did say that the Israeli kibbutzim are the perfect form of Communism whereas the Soviets have a modified communal system," I said.

"I didn't know that he said that, but that would be a hell of a good topic," Depue said.

Depue said Souther would enjoy discussing what he did with someone who is familiar with espionage.

Returning to Souther's tendency to choose the other side, Depue said, "People get attitudes toward life because of their relationship with their fathers. The father is an authority figure, and if he's an authoritarian type of person, the kid will get an attitude about authority in general from that."

In explaining his spying activity, Depue said, "I wouldn't so much say he's doing this to get back at his father. But he's developed this attitude as a result of his relationship with his father. He doesn't really know why he's doing that. It's a result of an attitude toward authority that is a result of his relationship toward his father. The attitude is one of resentment of authority.

"Here's a guy who is not going to be happy with anyone who makes him toe the line," he said. "He may not openly rebel. It's a kind of subtle sabotage. I wouldn't be surprised if you find that if he's mad at the boss, he'll scratch the guy's car rather than having a confrontation. He'll do little stuff. Maybe with his dad he would destroy his newspaper. It's retaliatory but indirect and weak. He's not a strong personality who says, 'Dad, I don't like this.' "

Such people can be candidates for suicide, Depue said.

"Suicide is the way a person who doesn't feel totally competent dies. It's almost a cowardly act," he said.[241]

32

Hey you!
Heaven!
Off with your hat!
I am coming!

—VLADIMIR MAYAKOVSKY, "A Cloud
  in Trousers"

AFTER NEARLY A YEAR of trying to obtain an interview with Souther, I received a letter from him from Moscow on June 3, 1989. In it Souther said he had received and read my letter, articles, and book [*Spy vs. Spy: Stalking Soviet Spies in America*] "with some interest." He claimed, however, that this was not because he found me an "exceptionally adept and intriguing writer," but because I wished "to invade [his] privacy."[242]

He continued that my having sent him what I'd written not only made him believe that I had "some kind of a love/hate relationship with the FBI," but that I was incapable of being objective in my conclusions. He wrote that based on the content of my letter to him, I had "already convicted [him] of espionage: guilty until proven innocent."

Citing these considerations, Souther said he felt an interview would only cause readers to "falsely believe that I agree to your conclusions in this new work." However, he offered to look at the manuscript so he could comment. Alternatively, he suggested that I might send him a list of questions that might allow for what Souther referred to as "some form of fair exchange of opinions" that he could respond to "in the quiet and calm of my home." This, he wrote, was the most he could do for me under what he referred to as "the present circumstances."

"Again," he concluded, "thank you for your very kind attention towards my life's vicissitudes."

I noted the sad tone of his last line. Defectors in either direction never have an easy time. They give up their family, their friends, their language, their culture, and their cuisine. All along, I had wondered if the Soviets had not allowed me to interview Souther because he was unstable or depressed. For someone who lived life as Souther had, the material deprivations of the Soviet Union would have been a shock. Even in the best hotels, one frequently cannot obtain a glass of milk or a piece of fruit. Because they get paid regardless of whether they take any fares, taxi drivers often refuse to pick up riders. And to buy an orange, a piece of meat, or a radio, one must stand in three lines—one to look at it, one to pay for it, and one to pick it out. Then the meat is largely fat, the orange still green.

One week of such grim conditions can be hell on an American. Three years of it would be unimaginable.

Souther's letter expressed an ambivalence that might mean he would consent to an interview. In a five-page, single-spaced letter, I wrote back to him that I am an independent journalist who has criticized the FBI when it has made mistakes:

> As for the question of your guilt or innocence, I propose to you that my opinion is irrelevant: What counts is how much substantiation can be cited, in the form of firsthand accounts, to show

that you engaged in spying activities such as the ones suggested
in my letter of March 30. Then what matters is how much coun-
tervailing information is presented to undercut that substantia-
tion.

Let me assure you that I am just as eager to present facts that
may exonerate you as I am to present ones that may indicate you
are guilty. I am not a prosecutor or FBI agent; I am an independent journalist. For example, while the *Time* excerpt did not include it, I extensively explored in *Moscow Station* the case of Marine
Staff Sergeant Robert M. Stufflebeam, who was believed by the
NIS to have been another spy at the embassy in Moscow. I showed
that he was not a spy and criticized the NIS for suggesting that
he was one.

I added that time was getting short. The manuscript for the
book was due soon. He would have to help speed up the process
for obtaining permission for me to interview him.

"If you could call or cable me collect, that would help," I
wrote. "If you have any other questions, please feel free to call
day or night."

My letter enclosed excerpts focusing on Souther's Russian
Club antics. It would have reached him by mid-June. Then on
June 27, 1989, the Soviet army newspaper *Red Star* reported
the bizarre news of his death in the obituary. Signed by the
ruling committee of the KGB, the obituary for Soviet intelligence officer Mikhail Yevgenyevich Orlov said he had died
suddenly at the age of thirty-two. In parentheses, the obituary
identified Orlov as Glenn Michael Souther.

Thus began the unprecedented disclosures by the Soviet
Union of his activities on behalf of the KGB, and the search to
determine if he had been a teenage mole. Never before had
the Soviets openly stated that a Westerner was a spy, as they
did in comparing Souther with Kim Philby and George Blake.
Nor had they ever suggested what kinds of material they re-

----

ceived from a spy, as they did in stating that Souther had had access to nuclear war plans and spy satellite photos.

After the Soviets cleared up the mystery of his origin by saying he had been born in the United States, the government newspaper *Izvestia* provided the first details of his death.

According to the paper, on June 22, 1989, Souther drove to his country house near Moscow and wrote notes to his mother, wife, daughter, and the KGB. Conspicuously missing from that list was his father. He then entered his garage, closed the door behind him, started up his Soviet-made Zhiguli car, and waited. He was found dead the next morning.

Souther had always admired Mayakovsky for shooting himself. He himself would have said that by asphyxiating himself, Souther had taken the coward's way out.

One of Souther's friends told *Pravda* that Souther immersed himself in work. "There were times when he plunged into depression, but nobody thought about the tragic outcome," the friend said.

The *Izvestia* article added that Souther had taken as his last name Orlov, the Russian name for eagle, because it symbolized strength and freedom. The newspaper promised that still more details would be revealed about Souther and his work for the Soviet Union. Indeed, shortly thereafter, *Pravda* quoted from Souther's suicide note: "Justice demands that you hear my last words. I do not regret our relationship. It was a long-standing one, and it helped me grow as a person. I wish to be buried in the uniform of an officer of the KGB."

It was a striking example of *glasnost* at work, only this time it was working in the opposite direction—against American interests. Indeed, the KGB's obvious delight in trumpeting Souther's success seemed like a throwback to the Cold War. The fact that *Izvestia* got several details wrong—claiming

Souther had been tried in the United States after he fled, for example—only added to that impression.[243]

The Soviets seemed to be sending several messages. One was that successful spies will be given a hero's welcome in the Soviet Union. Even if the Soviets did admit that Souther was unhappy there, the publicity ensured that the KGB would recruit more spies looking for their place in the sun. Another message was that the Soviet Union still has to be on guard against foreign penetration. The emphasis on America's nuclear war plans suggested that the United States could still be an aggressor. The third message was that the KGB's work is primarily directed against foreign spies rather than internal dissenters. For some time, the KGB under Soviet leader Mikhail Gorbachev had been emphasizing its foreign rather than its domestic role. Finally, the Souther case gave the Soviets something to rally around, something to be proud of. When sugar and meat are scarce, trumpeting the success of a spy is a good way to divert attention from the hardships of daily Soviet life.

The effect of the disclosures was to rub the noses of U.S. intelligence agencies in their own failures—always a good way to keep the other side on the defensive.

KGB chief Vladimir Kryuchkov, in explaining the publicity, reminded reporters of his promise in May 1989 to begin reporting regularly to the public on the intelligence agency's "major and important operations."

"The activities of our services will not be as secretive as they were until recently," he said then in an interview published on the front page of *Izvestia*. "While we will continue to observe our professional principles—without which our work is unthinkable—we will keep the public better informed about our work."[244]

It is never possible to determine with precision exactly what

----

material a spy divulged. Even when a spy confesses, as did John Walker, he cannot remember all the secrets he revealed. In Souther's case, no one on the U.S. side knows precisely what documents he gave away, and a defense lawyer could argue that there is no evidence he gave away anything. But when someone with a security clearance says he is working for the Soviets, admits to his former wife he received money from them, is seen by his girlfriend with large wads of cash that he says he got from a mysterious source, confides that the same source told him to take Russian and said he would protect him in the event of war between the United States and the U.S.S.R., engages in extensive spycraft, from tuning in coded shortwave radio messages to painting marks used by the KGB on bridges, defects to the Soviet Union, espouses Communism on Soviet television, is eulogized by the KGB as a Soviet hero, is said by *Pravda* to have sat in on nuclear war planning sessions and "compared details and selected the most important," is given the rank of major in the Soviet spy agency, is compared by *Pravda* to a legendary spy like Philby, and writes a suicide note to the KGB stating he has no regrets about his long-standing relationship with the spy agency, only a fool would cling to the idea that the Soviets were lying when they touted Souther as a spy comparable to Philby. While the Soviets never flatly said Souther gave them America's nuclear war plans, the fact that he had access to them, that they mentioned his access, and that they said he selected the most important facts about those plans would lead a reasonable person to conclude, against the background of his spy activities, that he gave the Soviets the plans.

In the Souther case, there was far more evidence that he was a successful spy than in the case of Edward Lee Howard, the former CIA employee who also defected to the Soviet Union. Nobody in the United States knows for sure what Howard gave the Soviets. But the fact that he knew key facts about important Soviets working for the CIA in Moscow, that Soviet defector Vitaly S. Yurchenko said Howard had been of immense help to the Soviets, that Howard defected to the Soviets, and that many of those important CIA assets were later caught and executed means Howard is widely assumed by the intelligence agencies and the media to have provided the Soviets with the identities of CIA assets in Moscow.

When a spy as resourceful as Souther had virtually unlimited access to one of the most sensitive posts in the U.S. military, counterintelligence experts assume he stole everything. Indeed, in reports that remain secret, the FBI concluded as much.

"If the material Souther was giving the Soviets was not of the best quality, he would have been scolded and not paid," said a senior intelligence official familiar with the case. "It may turn out that the Soviets' damage assessment is more accurate than our own," he said.

Meanwhile, the U.S. government was engaged in covering up the seriousness of the damage. Government spokesmen said he never had access to nuclear war plans. The cover-up extended to the previous investigations of Souther. *The Washington Times* was the first to mention that Souther's wife had tipped off the NIS to Souther's activities. The story said investigators dropped the probe after Souther's brother-in-law discounted the charges.[245]

In fact, there had been no investigation—not even a written report of her allegation.

A subsequent story in *The New York Times* said Souther's former wife told the NIS she believed Souther was a Soviet agent. The story said she was under the influence of alcohol when she met with NIS agents. According to the story, she declined to provide any details or to cooperate, and the investigation was dropped.[246]

The truth was that Di Palma approached the NIS agent at

a New Year's Eve party and that he never asked her for any details or for her cooperation.

The stories reflected the determination of the intelligence agencies to conceal the truth about the damage Souther had done and the subsequent bungling of the investigations. Because intelligence agencies operate in secrecy, it is that much easier for them to conceal their mistakes.

For Souther's friends from the Russian Club, the final development in his life came almost as an anticlimax. They had already suffered through the uncertainty of not knowing what had happened to him, then faced the shock of learning he had defected and was denouncing the United States. Many who knew him best had predicted he would become depressed in the Soviet Union. They were not surprised when they learned he had committed suicide.

Yet Danine Klein was surprised that she didn't cry.

"I feel sad, of course, but I don't know if it's because I feel all the grieving was done before, or that I got to hating him so much after he left and brought all this down on us," she said. "I'm glad he died because I don't see how his life was going to get any better, and he obviously wasn't happy the way it was. He had a star-crossed fate."[247]

Cindy saw the suicide as confirmation of "what was going on inside all this time—the depression and anguish and pain."[248]

"I think he did it because he was always for the underdog," she said. "When he started working for the U.S. government, he started finding out things the U.S. government was doing. It angered him. Nobody in the navy liked the Soviet Union. Because of his lack of self-esteem, he felt that by spying he could find purpose and meaning in his life."[249]

Di Palma had been hoping that Souther would communicate with their son, and she had given me a photograph of Angelo to give to him should I ever see him. I enclosed it in one of my letters to him, and he would have received it before his death.

Now Angelo would never know his father.

"I feel bad," Di Palma said. "I didn't want him to die."[250]

Later, Di Palma said she feared that Souther's family or friends would try to kill her for telling on him. It was a switch from the earlier situation, when Souther's family thought Di Palma's family had killed him.

"I made a mistake to talk to the FBI and to talk to you," she said. "Now I don't feel safe. I'm sure the parents think it's my fault. I don't know what they can do to me. Maybe friends would do something. I am afraid."[251]*

According to Tim Souther, his mother is mad at Di Palma for informing on her son.[252]

Besides his friends and family, Souther left behind a string of unanswered questions: How did he become interested in Communism? Did he feel any regrets about selling out his friends and family? Why did he feel that his only escape was through death?

They are unfathomable acts—spying against one's own country, defecting to a foreign power, then taking one's own life. If there are any answers, they can be found in the life and poems of Mayakovsky, the Russian poet whom Souther venerated. In Mayakovsky, Souther saw himself. In his poems, he saw a vindication of his own life.

Those poems reveal Mayakovsky as a split personality, a person who craved acclaim but also turned people away by outraging them; who was alternately cruel and gentle; who railed against bureaucracy and restrictions on freedom but also yearned for direction and order. He was a man who was alter-

---

*Although Di Palma's concerns were groundless, the author deleted from the book her location in Italy.

nately morose and exuberant. By turns, he was in constant pain and miserably lonely, yet able to give joy to others.

By his own account, Mayakovsky was a troubled, bored, lonely child growing up in the Georgian village of Baghdadi, where he was born in 1893. He found an answer at the age of twelve when he joined the Bolsheviks. The following year, his father died of an infection after he pricked his finger filing documents.[253] Three years later, Mayakovsky was arrested for collaborating with the Bolsheviks. He spent eleven months in prison.

After prison, he first dabbled in abstract painting, then turned to poetry. Quickly, he was embraced as the poet of the revolution, which he called "my revolution."

"Comrades, to the barricades!," he wrote. "Streets are our brushes,/squares our palettes!" Puns, thumping rhythms, grammatical deformations, and bold, brutal images became his signature.

"The young iconoclasts of Moscow were spellbound by him, respectable people were scandalized, while women of every sort found him irresistible," wrote Patricia Blake in an introduction to *The Bedbug and Selected Poetry*.[254]

Mayakovsky dressed in custom-tailored suits and wore his hair long and scruffy. Like Souther, he was compulsively neat, constantly washing his hands and cleaning and recleaning eating utensils.[255] And like Souther, he swooned over a succession of women and loved to boast of his success with them.

"The greatest pleasure is to wait in clean bedclothes for the arrival of the female species," he once told a friend. Yet he quickly left women who loved him too easily.

Despite a wide circle of friends in Russia's literary community, Mayakovsky perceived himself as a lonely, alienated individual. He loved animals because "they are not people, yet they are living creatures." Animal symbolism is an important part of his work.[256]

In 1916, Mayakovsky wrote: "I am as lonely as the single eye/of the one-eyed walking toward the blind."[257]

"The poet's lyric hero strives to overcome his loneliness," Alexander Ushakov wrote in *Vladimir Mayakovsky: Selected Verse*.[258] "He yearns toward people, hoping to find sympathy and support in them. 'For a single word, tender and humane,' he is prepared to give away all the treasures of his soul. But he is disappointed: Nobody needs or understands him."

In *The Way I Became a Dog*, Mayakovsky is driven to desperation by a bestial mob and turns into a dog, much as Souther acted doglike when nipping at the heels of waitresses. He yearns for an all-embracing lover, but when he finds it he remains alone and unhappy. In "A Cloud in Trousers," Maria, the object of his passion, rejects him for the sake of philistine well-being.

The same dichotomy ran through Mayakovsky's poetry. On the one hand, he trumpeted the values of conformity: "I want/ a commissar/with a decree/to lean over the thought of the age/ . . . I want/the factory committee/to lock/my lips/when the work is done," he wrote in "Back Home." But he also criticized mindless collectivism. In "About Conferences," he points out that at daybreak every office worker disappears into conferences of the "A,B,C,D,E,F,G committees re: the purchase of a bottle of ink by the provincial co-op." Annoyed that no one has returned to his desk by nightfall, Mayakovsky bursts into a conference, only to find torsos in attendance. A clerk informs him that the workers have had to split themselves up to meet organizational needs.

"Oh, for just one more conference re: the eradication of all conferences!" he wrote.[259]

During the two years before his death, Mayakovsky came to

understand the nature of the society he once applauded. He saw the conflict between the individual and the collective, the artist and the bureaucrat. In 1928, he wrote "The Bedbug," a devastating satire of Communist society. The poem highlights profiteers, party fat cats, and vodka-drenched bureaucrats.

The authorities received his new poems angrily. One critic stated in *Pravda* that Mayakovsky was emulating the Trotskyist opposition. While he claimed to be impervious to criticism, Mayakovsky was remarkably sensitive. He became enraged that his work was not appreciated, just as Souther became enraged at his navy superiors.

Much like Mayakovsky, Souther had become disillusioned with Soviet life, even though his suicide note expressed no regrets about his relations with the KGB. And just as the Soviets proclaimed Souther a star after his death, so had they heaped praise on Mayakovsky.

"Mayakovsky was and remains the best and most talented poet of our Soviet epoch," Stalin said after his death. Indeed, "Indifference to his memory and to his work is a crime," Stalin proclaimed. In case the force of law failed to enshrine his memory, his hometown was renamed for him, and a square in Moscow was dedicated to him. For an iconoclast, the official recognition would have been a bitter irony.

Four days before his death, an acquaintance ran into him. He pointed out that *Pravda* had revised its assessment of "The Bedbug" to a more positive one.

"Never mind. It's too late now," Mayakovsky responded.

On April 14, 1930, in observance of the Russian superstition that before death a man must put on clean linen, he changed his shirt. He placed a single cartridge in the cylinder of his revolver. Then he shot himself in the heart.[260]

Mayakovsky's suicide note, addressed "to all," said, "Do not blame anyone for my death, and please do not gossip. The deceased terribly disliked this sort of thing. Mama, sisters, and comrades, forgive me—this is not a way out (I do not recommend it to others), but I have none other . . . do not think me weak-spirited. Seriously, there was nothing else I could do. Greetings."[261]

He left behind a final verse:

> And, as they say, the incident is closed.
> Love's boat has smashed against the daily grind.
> Now life and I are quits. Why bother then
> to balance mutual sorrows, pains, and hurts.

Contradictory to the end, Souther had wanted to be buried in a uniform, even though he railed all his life against conformity and mindless bureaucracy. He had changed his last name to the Russian word for eagle—a symbol of America and freedom. His new middle name was the Russian form of Eugene: It was his father's first name, even though he had severed ties with him.

But Souther had achieved his lifelong ambition to be an officer—an officer of the KGB, as it turned out. At last he had become important, so important that the chief of the KGB called his death an "enormous loss." By taking his own life, he had achieved the ultimate manipulation, plunging his family and friends into sorrow while focusing the attention of the world on himself.

It was the final irony that in death Souther received the acclaim that had eluded him in life.

Epilogue

The universe sleeps,
its huge paw curled
upon a star-infested ear.

—VLADIMIR MAYAKOVSKY, "A Cloud
in Trousers"

THE ESPIONAGE INVESTIGATION of Souther is closed.

Greg Scovel has been neither fired, demoted, nor reprimanded for failing to follow up on Di Palma's allegation that Souther was working for the Soviets. He continues as a Naval Investigative Service agent based in Norfolk, Virginia.[262]

The Norfolk office of the FBI has blamed the mishandled interview with Souther on the NIS and the fact that it did not inform the Bureau of the truth about the original spy allegation. However, the FBI's counterintelligence division at headquarters has decided there was no excuse for not going back to Di Palma to interview her before confronting Souther.

Danine Klein is living in San Francisco and managing a restaurant while applying to graduate schools to obtain a Ph.D. in the Russian language.[263]

King Butterworth is a patient accounts representative at a hospital in Norfolk.[264]

248

Cindy is the manager of an electronics store in the Washington area. She is married and recently had a baby.[265]

Jon Berryman is a paralegal in Chicago.[266]

Bob Fitch is a navy engineer supervising ship construction in Bath, Maine. He recently got married.[267]

After Souther bit her, Cynthia Kotulak transferred from Old Dominion and realized her ambition to become a registered nurse.[268]

John Fahey has retired from Old Dominion University but continues to be active in Norfolk-area civic activities.[269] Leonid Mihalap continues to teach at Old Dominion.[270]

Patrizia Di Palma and her son, Angelo, are living with a medical doctor in Italy. She assists him in his work and, being a fabulous chef, he does the cooking.[271]

Angelo Souther has grown to be a handsome, exceptionally smart, sensitive, and outgoing boy. He has the same eyes, lips, and body structure as his father, but he does not remember him. "Before he would ask me about him all the time," Di Palma said. "He wanted to see pictures of him. I have very few."

Glenn Souther is buried near the legendary British spy Kim Philby in Novokuntsevskoye Cemetery in the western suburbs of Moscow. The cemetery is reserved for high-ranking KGB officers, distinguished Soviet citizens, and military personnel. According to General Vladimir Kryuchkov, the chief of the KGB, the suicide note he left behind expressed his appreciation to the Soviet Union for recognizing his services.

Notes

1. *Red Star*, June 27, 1989, page 4. Grateful appreciation is extended to John A. Fahey for translating this and other Soviet press articles.

2. Reuters, June 28, 1989.

3. *Ibid.*

4. *Los Angeles Times*, June 29, 1989.

5. *Pravda*, July 1, 1989.

6. Phillip Knightly, *The Master Spy* (Alfred A. Knopf, 1989), page 260.

7. *Newsweek*, August 21, 1989, page 28.

8. *Los Angeles Times*, July 2, 1989.

9. Vladimir Mayakovsky, with an introduction by Patricia Blake, *The Bedbug and Selected Poetry* (Indiana University Press, 1960), page 23.

10. Presentencing report on Souther of August 9, 1984, filed in Norfolk Circuit Court, Norfolk, Virginia.

11. Souther's parents and stepparents declined requests to be interviewed made by letter and by telephone over a period of a year.

12. Interview on October 2, 1988, with Petsas.

13. Interview on September 29, 1988, with Vitkus.

14. Interview on July 15, 1989, with Biter.

15. Interview on September 26, 1988, with Duggan.

16. Interview on September 28, 1988, with Eastwood.

17. Interview on September 27, 1988, with Vance.

18. Interview on June 30, 1989, with Rodenburg.

19. Interview on October 30, 1988, with Duggan.

20. Interview on November 11, 1988, with Edna Vance.

21. Interview on November 11, 1988, with Vance.

22. Interview on September 24, 1988, with Tim Souther.

23. Interview on September 21, 1988, with Tim Souther.

24. Interview on September 24, 1988, with Tim Souther and on January 20, 1989, with Di Palma. Both said they believe Wiergacz hit Souther once.

25. Obsessive-compulsive disorders, including those manifesting themselves in excessive sexual behavior, are defined in *Diagnostic and Statistical Manual of Mental Disorders* (American Psychiatric Association, 1987), page 245.

26. Interview on September 24, 1988, with Tim Souther.

27. Interview on April 3, 1989, with Bendixon.

28. Interview on October 22, 1988, with Cleveland.

29. *Ibid.*

30. Interview on October 6, 1988, with Fitch.

31. *Ibid.*

32. Interview on October 26, 1988, with Caine.

33. Interview on September 24, 1988, with Tim Souther.

34. Interview on October 6, 1988, with Fitch.

35. *Ibid.*

36. Interview on October 6, 1988, with Fitch.

37. Interview on April 3, 1989, with Bendixon.

38. Interview on January 20, 1989, with Di Palma.

39. *Ibid.*

40. *Ibid.*

41. *Ibid.*

42. *Ibid.*

43. Interview on January 20, 1989, with Di Palma.

44. *Ibid.*

45. Interview on May 20, 1989, with Di Palma.

46. Interview on January 20, 1989, with Di Palma.

47. *Ibid.*

48. *Ibid.*

49. Interview on January 21, 1989, with Di Palma.

50. Interview on January 22, 1989, with Di Palma.

51. Interview on January 20, 1989, with Di Palma.

52. Interview on January 22, 1989, with Di Palma.

53. Interview on January 20, 1989, with Di Palma.

54. Interview on January 20, 1989, with Di Palma, and on January 30, 1989, with an NIS agent. Scovel has claimed he asked Di Palma to call him and she never did, but he has admitted he did not follow up as he should have.

55. Interview on July 27, 1988, with an NIS official. Smallwood, on May 22, 1989, declined to comment. "You write what you want to write," he said.

56. Interview on January 20, 1989, with Di Palma.

57. Interview on July 27, 1988, with an NIS official.

58. Interview on January 22, 1989, with Di Palma.
59. Interview on July 27, 1988, with an NIS official.
60. *Old Dominion University Catalog*, 1988–90, page 1.
61. Interview on November 1, 1988, with Long.
62. Interview on October 28, 1988, with Cindy.
63. Interview on November 1, 1988, with Cindy.
64. *Ibid.*
65. Interview on September 21, 1988, with Tim Souther.
66. Interview on November 1, 1988, with Cindy.
67. Interview on October 28, 1988, with Cindy.
68. *Ibid.*
69. *Ibid.*
70. *Ibid.*
71. Interview on November 1, 1988, with Cindy.
72. Interviews on November 6, 1988, with Weiser and Graham.
73. Interview on November 6, 1988, with Weiser.
74. *Ibid.*
75. Interview on October 28, 1988, with Cindy.
76. Interview on August 3, 1988, with Klein.
77. Interview on August 3, 1988, with Fahey.
78. Interview on August 4, 1988, with Mihalap.
79. Interview on July 7, 1989, with Klein.
80. Interview on August 11, 1988, with Klein.
81. Interview on August 3, 1988, with Klein.
82. Interviews on August 12, 1988, and July 17, 1989, with Higger.
83. Interview on October 9, 1988, with Philips.
84. *Ibid.*
85. Interview on August 3, 1988, with Klein.
86. Interview on October 28, 1988, with Cindy.
87. Figures on Souther's income come from an August 9, 1984, presentencing report filed in Norfolk Circuit Court. The calculation of $419 a month for tuition is based on Old Dominion's rate at the time of $1,884 per semester for nonresident students, according to the bursar's office.
88. Interview on October 28, 1988, with Cindy.
89. *Ibid.*
90. *Ibid.*
91. Interview on November 1, 1988, with Cindy.
92. Interview on October 28, 1988, with Cindy.
93. Navy Information and Personnel Security Program Regulation, OPNAVINST 5510.1H, pages 21–1 through 21–3.
94. Interview on October 28, 1988, with Cindy.
95. *Ibid.*
96. *Ibid.*
97. *Ibid.*
98. *Ibid.*

99. Interview on August 3, 1988, with Klein.

100. Interview on October 28, 1988, with Cindy, and on August 3, 1988, with Klein.

101. Interview on December 30, 1988, with Kotulak.

102. *Ibid.*

103. Interview on August 3, 1988, with Klein.

104. Interview on December 30, 1988, with Kotulak.

105. Interview on November 14, 1988, with Lucas.

106. Interview on June 28, 1989, with Byrd.

107. Interview on June 3, 1989, with Fahey.

108. Interview on August 13, 1988, with Oberg.

109. Interview on December 30, 1988, with Kotulak.

110. Interview on August 19, 1988, with Talbott.

111. Interview on October 28, 1988, with Cindy.

112. Norfolk Circuit Court case #841055–MO4, and interview on May 3, 1989, with Judge Stewart.

113. *The Russian School of Norwich University Bulletin.*

114. Interview on August 3, 1988, with Klein.

115. *Ibid.*

116. Interview on September 16, 1988, with Berryman.

117. Interview on August 3, 1988, with Klein, and on August 30, 1988, with Butterworth. Dory declined comment.

118. Interview on August 3, 1988, with Klein.

119. Interview on September 16, 1988, with Berryman.

120. Interview on August 3, 1988, with Klein, and on September 16, 1988, with Berryman.

121. Interview on August 10, 1988, with Berryman.

122. Interview on September 16, 1988, with Berryman.

123. Interview on August 21, 1988, with Stout.

124. Interview on August 19, 1988, with Zauber.

125. *Fundamentals of Naval Intelligence* (Naval Education and Training Command, 1975), page 301.

126. William E. Burrows, *Deep Black* (Random House, 1986), page 19.

127. Department of the Navy Personnel Security Program Regulation, OPNAVINST 5510.1H, pages 14–1 through 14F–10, and interview on May 5, 1989, with a former officer assigned to FICEURLANT.

128. Department of the Navy Personnel Security Program Regulation, OPNAVINST 5510.1H, pages 10–1 through 10–3.

129. Interview on July 30, 1988, with a former naval officer.

130. Interview on August 30, 1988, with Hassencahl.

131. Interview on September 9, 1988, with Fisher.

132. *Ibid.*

133. *Ibid.*

134. Interview on September 4, 1988, with Goodbar.

135. Interview on August 3, 1988, with Fahey.

136. Interview on August 4, 1988, with Mihalap.

137. Article by Ebba R. Hierta in *The Day*, New London, Connecticut, July 24, 1988, page A-1, confirmed in an interview with Hierta.

138. *Love Is the Heart of Everything: Correspondence Between Vladimir Mayakovsky and Lili Brik, 1915–1930*, edited by Bengt Jangfeldt (Grove Press, 1986), page 34.

139. Interview on August 3, 1988, with Fahey.

140. Interview on August 30, 1988, with Sapozhnikov.

141. Interview on August 11, 1988, with Klein.

142. Interview on August 30, 1988, with Sapozhnikov.

143. *Ibid.*

144. The case of Karl F. Koecher and his wife, Hana, is discussed at length in the author's 1988 book, *Spy vs. Spy*, published by Scribner's.

145. *The Falcon and the Snowman*, a 1984 Orion Pictures release.

146. Interview on October 28, 1988, with Cindy.

147. *Ibid.*

148. Interview on November 1, 1988, with Long.

149. Interview on November 3, 1988, with Cindy.

150. Interview on October 6, 1988, with Fitch, and on the same date with Kinne.

151. Presentencing report of August 9, 1984, on Souther in Norfolk Circuit Court.

152. Interview on August 20, 1988, with Butterworth.

153. Interview on July 1, 1989, with Butterworth.

154. Interview on September 21, 1988, with Tim Souther.

155. Interview on August 20, 1988, with Butterworth.

156. Interview on August 21, 1988, with Stout.

157. Article by Hierta on page A-1, *The Day*, New London, Connecticut, July 24, 1988, confirmed in an interview with Hierta.

158. Interview on August 3, 1988, with Klein.

159. *Ibid.*

160. Interview on July 28, 1988, with a federal investigative source. McCay declined repeated requests to be interviewed, saying she wants to put the events behind her.

161. Interview on October 28, 1988, with Cindy.

162. The origins of the Walker case are discussed on pages 124–25 and 159–67 of the author's book *Spy vs. Spy*. In addition, John Barron's *Breaking the Ring* (Houghton Mifflin, 1987) gives an authoritative account of the FBI investigation of the case.

163. On May 24, 1989, Holtz declined to comment.

164. Interview on June 8, 1989, with Depue.

165. See the author's February 20, 1984, article in *The Washington Post*, page A-1.

166. Interview on June 8, 1989, with Depue.

167. *Ibid.*

168. The FBI's interrogation methods in espionage cases are discussed more fully on page 206 of the author's book *Spy vs. Spy*.

169. *Spy vs. Spy*, page 130.

170. Interview on August 3, 1988, with Klein.

171. Interview on July 16, 1989, with Hodge, and on July 18, 1989, with Dickinson.

----

172. Interview on May 22, 1989, with Carol Norton.

173. Interview on August 20, 1988, with Butterworth.

174. Interview on July 16, 1989, with Perrow.

175. Interview on June 26, 1989, with Hassencahl.

176. Interview on August 30, 1988, with Hassencahl.

177. Interview on July 16, 1989, with Hodge.

178. Interview on September 21, 1988, with Tim Souther.

179. *Ibid.*

180. Interview on July 28, 1988, with a federal investigative source.

181. Interview on October 9, 1988, and on May 22, 1989, with Philips.

182. Interview on September 21, 1988, with Tim Souther.

183. Interview on January 20, 1989, with Di Palma.

184. Interview on October 28, 1988, with Cindy.

185. Interview on September 28, 1988, with Cindy.

186. Souther's grandfather hung up when asked by phone for comment on November 3, 1988.

187. Interview on September 29, 1988, with a former naval intelligence officer.

188. Interview on July 30, 1988, with a former naval intelligence officer.

189. Interview on October 11, 1988, with Faurer.

190. Interview on August 24, 1988, with a former official in the CIA's Directorate of Science and Technology.

191. Cross-examination of Kerr, then the CIA's associate deputy director for intelligence, in *U.S.* v. *Samuel Loring Morison,* U.S. District Court, Baltimore, page 56.

192. Interview on November 21, 1988, with a former high-ranking naval intelligence official.

193. Interview on October 9, 1988, with Philips.

194. Interview on August 3, 1988, with Klein.

195. *Ibid.*

196. Interview on July 18, 1989, with Dickinson.

197. Interview on August 30, 1988, with Sapozhnikov.

198. Interview on November 3, 1988, with a federal investigative agent.

199. Interview on November 4, 1988, with a federal investigative agent.

200. The efforts to interview Templeton or obtain her comment began on September 29, 1988, with a letter to her requesting an interview. When that got no response, the author sent her another letter on October 11, 1988, asking that she call the author to discuss an interview. On October 21, 1988, Templeton's lawyer, Philip R. Melangton, Jr., responded in a letter that Templeton did not want to be interviewed because "it has been requested that she refrain from discussing the matter with anyone other than the proper agents of our government and, of course, her attorney" because of the "sensitivity of this matter of national security." On October 29, 1988, the author called Melangton to discuss the matter further and followed up with a letter on that date enclosing his latest book. On November 9, 1988, the author talked with Melangton again, and at his request, sent him copies of the photos planned for use in the book. On November 23, 1988, the author wrote Templeton with some additional points in favor of granting an interview. She responded by phone that she did not want to be

interviewed, saying she wanted to put it all behind her. On December 7, 1988, the author sent her summaries of material about her planned for use in the book. On January 25, 1989, the author sent her more summaries, including material from extensive interviews in Italy with Patrizia Di Palma, Souther's former wife. On March 24, 1989, the author flew to Indianapolis to try to talk with Templeton. They had a pleasant but uninformative discussion through her second-story window. On May 26, 1989, the author sent Templeton a letter with a final request for comment or corrections to summaries already sent. A copy also went to Melangton. Neither responded.

201. *Virginian-Pilot*, November 19, 1986, page A-1.

202. United Press International story in the November 10, 1986, editions of *The Washington Post*, page D-2.

203. Interview on July 16, 1989, with Hodge, and on July 18, 1989, with Dickinson.

204. Interview on August 3, 1988, with Klein.

205. Interview on October 28, 1988, with Cindy.

206. Interview on September 21, 1988, with Tim Souther.

207. Letter of June 6, 1989, from Walker to the author.

208. Interview on January 20, 1989, with Di Palma, and on May 19, 1989, with a retired federal agent.

209. Interview on January 20, 1989, with Di Palma.

210. *Recent Espionage Cases* (Department of Defense Security Institute, February 1989). Besides Walker, Walker's brother, his son, and his friend Jerry Whitworth, the navy and marine corps personnel prosecuted are Lee E. Madsen, a navy yeoman, who was arrested and convicted for selling classified information to an FBI agent; Stephen Baba, a navy ensign, who was arrested and convicted for sending classified documents to the South African embassy in Washington; Brian E. Slavens, a marine corps private first class, who pleaded guilty to offering military information to the Soviet embassy in Washington; Brian P. Horton, a navy intelligence specialist who worked at FI-CEURLANT and attempted to sell information about SIOP to the Soviets; Hans P. Wold, stationed aboard the aircraft carrier U.S.S. *Ranger*, who was convicted of possessing top-secret information which he planned to give to the Soviets; John R. Maynard, a navy seaman, who was convicted after a search of his locker while he was on unauthorized leave disclosed fifty-one top-secret documents; Robert W. Ellis, a navy petty officer, who was convicted of offering to sell classified documents to the Soviet consulate in San Francisco; Jeffrey Pickering, a navy petty officer, who was convicted of sending a classified document to the Soviet embassy in Washington; Bruce L. Kearn, a navy operations specialist, who was convicted of delivering classified information to an unspecified nation; Robert E. Cordrey, a marine private, who was convicted of attempting to contact Soviet and Eastern bloc embassies in an effort to sell information on biological and chemical warfare; Samuel L. Morison, a civilian analyst with the Office of Naval Intelligence, who was convicted of supplying Jane's Publications with classified spy-satellite photos; Jay C. Wolff, a former navy enlisted man, who pleaded guilty to offering to sell to an undercover agent classified documents dealing with U.S. weapons systems aboard a U.S. naval vessel; Michael Tobias, a navy petty officer third class, who was convicted of stealing top-secret cryptographic cards from the U.S S.

Peoria and attempting to sell them to Soviet representatives; Jonathan J. Pollard, an intelligence analyst with the Naval Investigative Service, who was convicted of selling an entire roomful of classified documents to Israeli intelligence officials; Robert D. Haguewood, a navy petty officer third class, who pleaded guilty to selling part of an aviation ordnance manual to an undercover police officer; Michael H. Allen, a retired navy senior chief radioman, who was convicted of passing classified documents to Philippine intelligence officers; Clayton J. Lonetree, a marine corps security guard at the American embassy in Moscow, who was convicted of passing names of CIA officers and other classified material to a KGB officer posing as the "uncle" of a Soviet woman in the embassy; Wilredo Garcia, a navy master-at-arms first class, who was convicted of trying to sell classified documents to a foreign government, probably in the Eastern bloc; David Fleming, a navy chief petty officer, who was convicted of stealing secret photographs and training manuals; Henry O. Spade, a former navy radio operator, who was convicted of having unauthorized possession of top-secret documents; and Craig D. Kunkle, a former navy chief petty officer, who is being prosecuted for trying to sell classified antisubmarine warfare documents to the Soviets.

211. Active duty military personnel are as of September 30, 1988, according to the Defense Department public affairs office.

212. A fuller discussion of NIS investigative shortcomings in the counterintelligence area appears in the author's 1989 book, *Moscow Station*, published by Scribners, pages 193–96.

213. Interview on October 14, 1988, with an NIS official.

214. Interview on May 30, 1989, with a senior intelligence official.

215. U.S. Navy response to the author's questions of May 31, 1989.

216. *Washington Post*, November 1, 1988, page A-17, quoting a House Select Committee on Intelligence report.

217. A fuller discussion of the role of agency security breaches in spy cases appears in the author's book *Spy vs. Spy*, page 280.

218. Interview on November 21, 1988, with a retired naval intelligence official.

219. The *Izvestia* article of July 17, 1988, is quoted in the *Virginian-Pilot*, July 18, 1988, page A-1.

220. English translation by the Foreign Broadcast Information Service (FBIS) of "Camera Looks at the World," July 19, 1988, and a videotape of the program.

221. Interview on September 24, 1988, with Tim Souther.

222. *Washington Post*, July 18, 1988, page A-1.

223. Interview on May 31, 1989, with Tim Souther.

224. *Washington Post*, July 22, 1988, page A-22.

225. *New York Times*, April 9, 1989, page A-20.

226. *Washington Post*, August 3, 1984, page A-2, and interview on June 1, 1989, with Hentzel and on May 30, 1989, with a spokesperson for the U.S. Selective Service System.

227. Interview on May 2, 1989, with a spokesperson for the U.S. Selective Service System and on June 14, 1989, with a spokesperson for the Marriott Corporation.

228. Interview on December 30, 1988, with Kotulak.

----

229. Interview on August 30, 1988, with Butterworth.

230. Interview on August 3, 1988, with Klein.

231. Interview on August 11, 1988, with Klein.

232. Interview on November 12, 1988, with Tim Souther.

233. Interview on September 24, 1988, with Tim Souther.

234. Interview on October 29, 1988, with Tim Souther.

235. Interview on January 21, 1989, with Di Palma.

236. Interview on January 22, 1989, with Di Palma.

237. Interview on June 3, 1989, with Fahey.

238. Interview on August 10, 1988, with Berryman.

239. Interview on June 8, 1989, with Depue.

240. Interview on July 14, 1989, with Feshbach. The UCLA study was based on surveys of seven hundred people.

241. Interview on July 7, 1989, with Depue. Depue did not then know how Souther had died.

242. Letter of May 17, 1989, to the author from Souther.

243. *Izvestia*, June 29, 1989, page 6.

244. *Washington Post*, May 6, 1989.

245. *Washington Times*, June 28, 1989, page A-1.

246. *New York Times*, June 29, 1989.

247. Interview on June 28, 1989, with Klein.

248. Interview on June 28, 1989, with Cindy.

249. Interview on July 9, 1989, with Cindy.

250. Interview on June 28, 1989, with Di Palma.

251. Interview on July 2, 1989, with Di Palma.

252. Interview on July 20, 1989, with Tim Souther.

253. Victor Pertsov, *Vladimir Mayakovsky: Poems* (Moscow: Progress Publishers, 1972), page 8.

254. *The Bedbug and Selected Poetry*, edited by Patricia Blake, page 19.

255. Edward J. Brown, *Mayakovsky: A Poet in the Revolution* (Princeton University Press, 1973), page 28.

256. *Love Is the Heart of Everything: Correspondence Between Vladimir Mayakovsky and Lili Brik, 1915–1930*, page 18.

257. Herbert Marshall, *Mayakovsky* (Hill and Wang, 1965), page 26.

258. *Vladimir Mayakovsky: Selected Verse*, foreword by Alexander Ushakov (Moscow: Raduga Publishers, 1985), page 12.

259. *Ibid.*, page 32.

260. *The Complete Plays of Vladimir Mayakovsky*, translated by Guy Daniels (Washington Square Press Inc., 1968), page 16.

261. *Vladimir Mayakovsky: Selected Verse*, page 47.

262. Interview on June 28, 1989, with an NIS agent.

263. Interview on June 27, 1989, with Klein.

264. Interview on May 30, 1989, with Butterworth.

265. Interview on November 1, 1988, with Cindy.

266. Interview on June 27, 1989, with Berryman.
267. Interview on July 1, 1989, with Fitch.
268. Interview on December 30, 1988, with Kotulak.
269. Interview on June 28, 1989, with Fahey.
270. Interview on July 10, 1989, with Mihalap.
271. Interview on May 20, 1989, with Di Palma.

Navy Statement

The following are the U.S. Navy's responses to the author's questions:

Q. Does the navy take security as seriously as the other services?

A. There is no way to compare in quantifiable terms each service's commitment to security. The navy sees proper security measures as absolutely vital to meet its responsibilities in the defense of the United States. The responsibility for compliance with these measures rests with each individual member of the navy family, up and down the chain of command. The navy goes to great lengths to ensure that this compliance is forthcoming. Constant command attention and continuing security education have raised the overall awareness of this responsibility.

Q. What security changes involving security clearances and

access to spaces within intelligence commands have been made since the Walker and Souther cases?

A. Since 1985 a number of changes have been made in the navy's policies and practices concerning information and personnel security. Reforms and improvements in physical and technical security were implemented as well. Some predate the revelations of the Walker case and the Souther incident, and many are in direct response to the Stilwell Commission [recommendations] in November 1985.

▪ In March 1985, the chief of naval operations directed the consolidation of all navy "security-related" functions in one official, now known as the commander, Naval Investigative Service Command. The incumbent, Rear Admiral John E. Gordon, a two-star flag officer, is designated as the special assistant for naval investigative matters and security. For the first time, one official is responsible for *and* has authority over the policies governing law enforcement, physical security, criminal investigations, counterintelligence, and information and personnel security.

▪ Since then, the navy has overhauled its personnel security clearance adjudication system, withdrawing from commanders and commanding officers the authority to grant clearances. There is now a Department of the Navy Central Adjudication Facility which has assumed the consolidated responsibilities for performing records adjudication for all members of the navy family—active duty, reserve, and civilian.

▪ Consistent standards of quality are being applied throughout the Department of the Navy to the decision-making process in granting security clearances. Centralized adjudication means that the same organization is responsible for overseeing, granting, and policing security clearances for all hands. This means that the adjudicators have access to all officially recorded information concerning cleared personnel, including level of

----

clearance held. They know what prior investigations were conducted, whether they are due for periodic reinvestigation, and whether they are sufficient for the level of clearance and access granted. Adjudicators will know when naval personnel arc duc for periodic reinvestigation and whether they have been involved in a reported security violation. This will prevent a future John Walker from evading the security investigation and review process.

▪ Congress has approved the limited use of the polygraph as a condition of continuing access to classified information in specially designed top-secret and special-access programs. The navy expanded this program (with congressional approval) from thirty-nine examinations in fiscal year 1984 to 3,573 in fiscal year 1988.

▪ Today, the navy requires continued evaluation of cleared personnel. This is a joint effort, actively involving individuals, the command, the counterintelligence elements of the Naval Investigative Service, and the Department of the Navy Central Adjudication Facility.

▪ Navy policy requires inspection for classified material when persons enter and leave naval activities. Portal inspections are now commonplace at many navy buildings and facilities.

Naval Intelligence Glossary

ANALYSIS   The process of evaluating the significance of new information, either by itself or in conjunction with other pieces of information, in the context of current events or developments with the perspective of past experience relevant to the subject.

BASIC INTELLIGENCE   That factual intelligence which results from the collation of encyclopedic information of a fundamental and more or less permanent nature and which, as a result of evaluation and interpretation, is determined to be the best available.

CAPABILITY   The ability to execute a specified course of action.
CLANDESTINE OPERATIONS   Activities to accomplish intelligence, counterintelligence, and other similar activities sponsored or

conducted by governmental departments or agencies in such a way as to assure secrecy or concealment.

COLLECTION   The selection and allocation of operational and intelligence resources to collect against general and specific targets in response to identified intelligence requirements, the satisfaction of which is necessary to support all levels of command. Collection encompasses management of all types of resources, whether electronic, photographic, or human. Collection is also the actual process of obtaining required information.

COMBAT INTELLIGENCE   Knowledge of enemy weather and geographical features required by a commander in the planning and conduct of combat operations.

COMPARTMENTATION   Establishment and management of an intelligence organization so that information about the personnel, organization, or activities of one component is made available to any other component only to the extent required for the performance of assigned duties.

COUNTERESPIONAGE   A category of counterintelligence, the objective of which is the detection and neutralization of foreign espionage.

COUNTERINTELLIGENCE   Encompasses the neutralization of intelligence and collection efforts directed against the U.S. and identification of individuals, groups, activities, and/or movements, the objectives of which are inimical to the interests of the U.S. and specifically the U.S. Navy. The object of this functional area is to protect naval facilities and personnel from espionage, subversion, and sabotage.

COUNTERSABOTAGE   Action designed to destroy the effectiveness of foreign sabotage activities through the process of identifying, penetrating, and manipulating, neutralizing, or repressing individuals, groups, or organizations conducting or capable of conducting such activities.

COUNTERSUBVERSION A part of counterintelligence devoted to destroying the effectiveness of inimical subversive activities through the detection, identification, exploitation, penetration, manipulation, deception, and repression of individuals, groups, or organizations conducting or capable of conducting such activities.

COVERT OPERATIONS Operations which are so planned and executed as to conceal the identity of or permit plausible denial by the sponsor. They differ from clandestine operations in that emphasis is placed on concealment of identity of sponsor rather than on concealment of the operation.

CRITICAL INTELLIGENCE Information indicating a situation or pertaining to a situation which affects the security interests of the U.S. to such an extent that it may require the immediate attention of the President.

CURRENT INTELLIGENCE Intelligence of all types and forms of immediate interest which is usually disseminated without the delays incident to complete evaluation or interpretation.

DEPARTMENTAL INTELLIGENCE Intelligence relating to activities or conditions within the U.S. which threaten internal security and which might require the employment of troops, and intelligence relating to activities of individuals or agencies potentially or actually dangerous to the Department of Defense.

ELICITATION INTELLIGENCE Acquisition of information from a person or group in a manner which does not disclose the intent of the interview or conversation.

ESPIONAGE Actions directed toward the acquisition of information through clandestine operations.

ESSENTIAL ELEMENTS OF INFORMATION The critical items of information regarding the enemy and his environment needed by the commander by a particular time, to relate to other available information and intelligence in order to assist him in reaching a logical decision.

ESTIMATIVE INTELLIGENCE   That intelligence which assesses a foreign situation, development, or trend, and which identifies its major elements, interprets its significance, and appraises the future possibilities and the prospective results of the various actions that might be taken.

EVALUATION INTELLIGENCE   Appraisal of an item of information in terms of credibility, reliability, pertinence, and accuracy.

FOREIGN INTELLIGENCE   Intelligence concerning areas not under the control of the power sponsoring the collection effort.

INDICATIONS INTELLIGENCE   Information in various degrees of evaluation, all of which bears on the intention of a potential enemy to adopt or reject a course of action.

INFORMATION INTELLIGENCE   Unevaluated material of every description, including that derived from observations, reports, rumors, imagery, and other sources which, when processed, may produce intelligence.

INTEGRATION   The process of forming an intelligence pattern through selection and combination of evaluated information.

INTELLIGENCE   The product resulting from the collection, evaluation, analysis, integration, and interpretation of all information concerning one or more aspects of foreign countries or areas, which is immediately or potentially significant to the development and execution of plans, policies, and operations.

INTELLIGENCE ANNEX   A supporting document of an operation, plan, or order which provides detailed information on the enemy situation, assignment of intelligence tasks, and intelligence administrative procedures.

INTELLIGENCE COLLECTION PLAN   A plan for gathering infor-

----

mation from all available sources to meet an intelligence requirement. Specifically, a logical plan for transforming the essential elements of information into orders or requests to sources within a required time limit.

INTELLIGENCE ESTIMATE An appraisal of the elements of intelligence relating to a specific situation or condition with a view to determining the courses of action open to the enemy or potential enemy and the probable order of adoption.

INTELLIGENCE PROCESS The intelligence process (also intelligence cycle) consists of the steps by which information is assembled and converted into intelligence and the resulting product made available to users. These steps are generally grouped into three phases: collection, production, and dissemination.

OPERATIONAL INTELLIGENCE The day-to-day collection, evaluation, and dissemination of intelligence in direct support of national level commanders and operational commands.

OVERT OPERATION The collection of intelligence openly, without concealment.

SABOTAGE An act with an intent to injure, interfere with, or obstruct the national defense of a country by willfully injuring or destroying, or attempting to injure or destroy, any national defense or war material, premises, or utilities.

STRATEGIC INTELLIGENCE Intelligence which is required for the formation of policy and military plans at national and international levels.

SUBVERSION Action designed to undermine the military, economic, psychological, or political strength of a regime.

Source: Edited version of "The Language of Intelligence," *Fundamentals of Naval Intelligence*, Naval Education and Training Command, U.S. Navy.

TACTICAL INTELLIGENCE   Intelligence which is required for the planning and conduct of tactical operations. Essentially, tactical intelligence and strategic intelligence differ only in scope, point of view, and level of employment.

TARGET INTELLIGENCE   Intelligence which portrays and locates the components of a target or target complex and indicates its vulnerabilities and relative importance.

Source: Edited version of "The Language of Intelligence," *Fundamentals of Naval Intelligence*, Naval Education and Training Command, U.S. Navy.

Index